Take A
BREAK

I0479914

INDIA · SINGAPORE · MALAYSIA

Notion Press

No. 8, 3rd Cross Street,
CIT Colony, Mylapore,
Chennai, Tamil Nadu – 600 004

First Published by Notion Press 2020
Copyright © Priya Nair & Stonica Christie 2020
All Rights Reserved.

ISBN 978-1-64983-735-6

Take A BREAK

A Unique Experience
with Management Best-sellers

Priya Nair & Stonica Christie

INDIA · SINGAPORE · MALAYSIA

IND**IC**ACADEMY

INDIC PLEDGE

————◆◆————

- *I celebrate our civilisational identity, continuity & legacy in thought, word and deed.*

- *I believe our indigenous thought has solutions for the global challenges of health, happiness, peace and sustainability.*

- *I shall seek to preserve, protect and promote this heritage and in doing so,*
  - *discover, nurture and harness my potential,*
  - *connect, cooperate and collaborate with fellow seekers,*
  - *advance diversity and inclusivity in the society.*

ABOUT INDIC ACADEMY

————◆◆————

Indic Academy is a non-traditional 'university' for traditional knowledge. We seek to bring about a global renaissance based on Indic civilizational and indigenous thought. We are pursuing a multidimensional strategy across time, space and cause by establishing centers of excellence, transforming intellectuals and building an ecosystem.

Indic Academy is pleased to support this book.

Contents

With over 6,40,000 copies sold, **Goals!** by Brian Tracy, is a classic on how to set and achieve goals. It has been translated in more than twenty languages. Brian has more than seventy books to his credit out of which **Goals!** is amongst the most popular ones.

Aligned Thinking by Jim Steffen offers a transformational journey in making every moment count. This book has been converted to a program which has benefited numerous people over the last 35 years.

Richard J. Leider and David A. Shapiro's book **Work Reimagined** is a Silver Nautilus Award Recipient. It is a unique book that helps you uncover your career "calling". Richard and David have 10 and 6 books to their credit respectively.

Bringing a fresh perspective in having courage in all you do and having a career backbone, is Bill Treasurer's **Courage Goes To Work.** Having authored 6 books, this book has been translated into two languages

David A. Shapiro's **Choosing the Right Thing to Do** is a
moral guide to help you make decisions when posed with
troubling choices. It has been translated into four languages.
David A. Shapiro is the author and co-author of six books.

Collaborating with the Enemy by Adam Kahane showcases
an elaborate guide on how to work with people you don't like
or agree with. His works have been praised by Nobel Peace
Prize winners Nelson Mandela and Juan Manuel Santos.
Adam has four books to his credit.

A true story of Rocky Flats' environmental disaster turned into
Leading Extraordinary Performance, **Making the Impossible
Possible** was penned down by Kim Cameron & Marc Lavine.
This is one of Kim's fourteen books and Mark's first.

Get There Early takes leadership on the next level with
sensing the future and acting today to reach the right place
earlier than your competition. Written by Bob Johansen, this
book has been translated into four languages. This is one of
Bob's seven books

The Empress Has No Clothes by Joyce Roché & Alexander
Kopelman is an empowering book for Conquering Self-Doubt
to Embrace Success. Joyce is the author of three books, and
Alexander has ten books to his credit.

Revolving around the theme of What You Are Best at Could
Be Your Biggest Problem is the book **Fear Your Strengths**,
authored by Robert E. Kaplan & Robert B. Kaiser. Kaplan and
Kaiser have 19 and 3 books to their credit respectively.

About Us

Priya Nair

Priya, is an active social worker, associated with an NGO for the past 21 years. She holds a degree in Industrial Psychology and Masters in Social Work. Her passion of knowing and understanding what tickles the head and heart made her further deep dive in the area of Guidance and Counselling.

Child Rights, Women Empowerment, and issues related to Health have been her forte. She has worked extensively in these areas and made commendable contributions for the well-being of the underprivileged.

An avid reader and a flair for writing, paved way for this very thoughtful endeavour, and 'Take A Break' was born. What better way can be to return the favour to the society and create an impact on young minds in short pace of time.

Stonica Christie

Stonica is a curious millennial, with a passion for writing and reading, co-authored her first break with Priya. Coming from a very humble academician family, continuous learning has been her constant pursuit.

A Gold medallist in Human Resources, she was quick to realise the truth of corporate business. 'Take A Break' was a realisation, when she decided to pen down her thoughts about the corporate world. She decided to see corporate with a different perspective giving thumbs down to the cliché world.

Bold, courageous and willing to make a difference, makes her a very promising and enterprising professional. This creation is very close to her beliefs and ideals.

Berrett-Koehler Publishers

This book could not have been possible without the kind support of the Berrett-Koehler Team for granting us permission to summarize the books.

Their mission of Connecting People and Ideas to Create a World That Works For All has set them apart to be one of a kind. Changing lives, organizations and communities, BK believes that, to truly create a better world we need to take action on every level.

Working on their ideals, we approached Ms. Kate Piersanti, Copyrights Editor, BK group who helped us in getting our first break and supported us with her guidance.

We are forever grateful.

Preface

Thank you for picking up this book. We hope that this book helps you as much as it's helped us. Creating this piece has been a real joy, and we hope you enjoy this book too.

We have had the chance to meet a lot of working professionals, and being working professionals ourselves, the race against time had always been there. Juggling between work and home, we would miss out on that thing we really liked doing........ 'Reading'.

If we were facing these problems, surely others would also be in the same boat. Had read it somewhere in a study that the average number of books an avid reader reads in a year is 12. So what's your count?

We started thinking that how unfair it was to have huge reservoirs of knowledge out there and not being able to browse through them in the nick of time.

And that's how *Take A Break* happened. Collection of management best-sellers in brief.

With the summary compilation you would know the essence and heart of ten books; amazing right? And this doesn't end here, the collection is such that along with working professionals it will also be a read for all youngsters to expand their horizons and think from a holistic perspective.

Struggle with a choice to read one or none, against the choice of reading ten with the similar time investment.

Proven Methods, Success Stories & Practical Examples: three primary takeaways we look forward to from any book we read. Also the only things that we do remember. It's called hitting right at the sweet spot. This book has exactly the elixir to give to you from bestseller books.

So here's wishing you a Happy Reading Experience.

Introduction

This book is a culmination of top-notch lessons and a box of surprises from the world of management. While this book was underway, there was a lot of thought put into the chapters that would be included. To make it very holistic and useful, we decided to start off with the basics and then move ahead.

As you progress, you will find the topics in sync with one another and also interrelated. All these books have one thing in common and that is individual learning and development. Before starting off let's have a quick roundabout on what we will cover in this book.

We decided to start off with the books **Goals!** and **Aligned Thinking,** the action-oriented capsules. Setting goals and knowing how to achieve them. Making every moment count by identifying the high priority work areas. Important insights that will showcase your deliverables at work.

Once we've covered the basics, **Work Reimagined** focuses on helping you to find your calling. To uncover the reason of your being. A tough question all of us need to answer.

Courage Goes to Work and **Choosing the Right Thing To Do** revolve around work ideals. Having courage in everything you do and not being complacent. On the other side deciding between the right and wrong. Both books delve upon the choices you will need to make every single moment.

The Book **Collaborating with the Enemy** shows us the path of coordinating and adapting with the unlike-minded people in your work life. As life may have it you won't always get to work with people that you like and trust, the majority of the time it will be otherwise.

Next up, **Making the Impossible Possible** and **Get There Early** encompass new-age leadership skills. Changing the game with innovative vision. The lessons here will help you see things from different perspectives.

Conquering self-doubt and acknowledging success, **The Empress Has No Clothe**s is a special woman's perspective on women in corporates.

Playing by your strengths and their overuse can lead to a pitfall. **Fear Your Strengths** gives you real-life examples of how to direct your strengths for the best.

The prescribed way to read this book is to start off anytime you want to. Along the way, you will come across a lot of lessons and real-life examples. One by one you can start applying the same to your life as well and see the difference.

Good Luck and get started!

01

Goals!

About the Author
(Brian Tracy)

Brian Tracy is a Canadian-American motivational speaker and self-development author. With more than seventy books under his belt his works have helped people achieve personal and business goals easier and faster.

Brian has an enriched experience of 30 years in studying, researching, writing and speaking on subjects like economics, business, history, philosophy and psychology.

He has also consulted more than 1,000 companies worldwide. His corporate seminars on personal and professional development have aided in immediate changes and long-term results. Prior to finding his company, Brian Tracy International, Brian was the COO of a million-dollar development company.

He is active in community and national affairs and is the President of three companies headquartered in Solana Beach, California.

Goals!, Published by Berrett-Koehler Publishers; 2010

Goals!

Albert Einstein once said, "Imagination is more important than facts."

Going forward from this one thought, what one great thing would you dare to dream if you knew you could not fail? If you could be absolutely guaranteed of successfully achieving any goal, large or small, short term or long term, what one goal would it be? If you can write down your answer to these questions, you are probably going to achieve it. From that point onwards, the only question you ask yourself is, **"How?"** The intensity of how badly you want it is going to decide the limit of your hard work, your perseverance and dedication.

Quite often we notice that very few people set goals. What is more intriguing is why majority of them don't set goals? Why do people find it very difficult to set goals? The four primary reasons are:

- Goals Aren't Important – Very large section of our population belongs to that section of social structure, where goals are not part of their daily life. Even if an individual has any goal, they neither get discussed nor valued.

- They Don't Know How – Another section of our population is unaware of how to set Goals. They commonly mistake Goals for fantasies and wishful thinking, say for example like "want to be happy."
- The Fear of Failure – Then there is fear of failure, because failure hurts. It is very painful. It is financially and emotionally draining. Lot of people find it difficult to fight back, and they just give it up as a lost cause.
- The Fear of Rejection – The social stigma of failure is a huge burden for people to carry. It is always at the back of my mind that if I set a goal and fail then I am up for a lot of unnecessary criticism.

While all of the above are prominent reasons why people don't set goals, what most of them fail to understand is that whatever you need in life, big or small, requires Goals. Even if it is for wishful thinking like "I want to be happy" you need to answer the most important question, **"How?"**.

Goals give you a sense of meaning and purpose, a sense of direction. Goals make you feel happier and stronger, energized and effective, confident and competent. It enables you to control the direction of your life.

What gets in our way of achieving our goals is what you need to understand, reflect, fight and conquer. The biggest and the worst enemy and roadblock between you and your goals is **Negativity**. It continuously nags you from your positive moves. It distracts you with feelings of failure, rejection, criticism and limits you to mediocrity. It pulls you down, tires you out and makes your environment gloomy, dull and lifeless. It makes you hostile, irritable and unpleasant.

Let us understand the importance of having control of our own life with this example. Imagine for a moment that your life is like any other organization, where there are multiple factors, roles and responsibilities assigned to each segment for the continuance of the business. Remember, like in organizations, you are the sole owner of your most important organization, your life. You are responsible for its marketing, packaging and promoting it in this competitive market. Just like you put in hard work for your organization, you need to put in the same or more for your own life. Like business has goals, plans and objectives, you are also obligated towards your life. When you work hard in your organization, its value goes up, people start respecting and its reflection is seen through stock price. Your story is no different. If you work more, are more productive, more effective, then there are more takers. But if it is the other way round, then like people dump stocks of non-performing organizations, they will dump you also. Therefore along with ambition comes more responsibility. The more you take the happier you become.

Self-limiting belief is a crime. You become what you think about most of the time. Leaders think about the future, what they want and what can be done to achieve it. With self-limiting beliefs you consider yourself to be inadequate in intelligence, ability, talent, creativity and personality. You underestimate yourself and you set either no goals or low goals.

Charles Garfield made an interesting discovery of "Blue Sky Thinking". You look up to the blue sky and you realize everything is possible and the world is limitless. When you practice this you start moving into the future and you don't start compromising on small goals or half success. "Just do it" becomes your motto and you find yourself in the driver seat, as an action-oriented high achiever.

Aristotle said that the ultimate aim of human life is to achieve your own happiness. You are the very happiest when what you are doing on the outside is congruent with your values on the inside. Your goals and values must be complementing to each other and when they do not, it creates stress, unhappiness and pessimism.

In the Bible it says, "What does it benefit a man if he achieves the whole world but loses his own soul?" The happiest people in the world today are those who are living in harmony with their innermost convictions and values. The unhappiest people are those who are attempting to live incongruent with what they truly value and believe.

Trusting your intuition, watching your behavior and examining your past are some of the insightful things that will help you determine your core values. A spiritual teacher Emmet Fox talked about heart's desire, "How would you like to be remembered?" Psychologists have discovered: The more your behavior is consistent with what you feel your ideal behavior should be, the more you like and respect yourself, and the happier you are. "Integrity is not so much a value in itself; it is rather the value that guarantees all the other values."

Truly great men and women are always described as having high levels of integrity. They live their lives with highest values, even when no one is looking; on the other hand, the mediocre are always cutting corners and compromising their integrity. Always live in truth with yourself and others.

Once you accept complete responsibility for your life, you are ready to take-off.

Henry David Thoreau once wrote, "Have you built your castles in the air? Good. That is where they should be built. Now, go to work and build foundations under them." In determining your true goals, you start with your vision, your values and your ideals.

To set clear goals, you must focus on Clarity. Clarity leads to the definite purpose. As Napoleon Hill says, "There is one quality which one must possess to win, and that is definiteness of purpose, the knowledge of what one wants and a burning desire to possess it." Your reticular cortex is a special organ within the brain that contains your reticular activating system. For example, imagine that you decided that you wanted a red sports car. You write this down as a goal. You begin to think about and visualize a red sports car. This process sends the message to your reticular cortex that a "red sports car" is now important to you. This picture immediately goes up onto your mental radar screen. From that moment onward, you will start to notice red sports cars wherever you go.

"The only thing that stands between a man and what he wants from life is often merely the will to try it and the faith to believe that it is possible." – Richard M. DeVos

Your self-concept precedes and predicts your levels of performance and effectiveness in everything you do. Everything that you accomplish in your outer world is a result of your self-concept.

Thomas Edison was expelled from school in the 6th Grade. His parents were told that it would be a waste of time to spend any money educating him, because he was not particularly smart or capable of being taught anything. Edison went on to become the greatest inventor of the modern age.

As the saying on the wall of the inner city school reads, "God don't make no junk." Each person is capable of achieving excellence in some way, in some area. You have within you, right now, the ability to function at genius or exceptional levels in at least one and perhaps several different intelligences. Your job is to find out what it could be for you. Top people look for the good in every situation. They expect to get something good out of everything that happens to them. They believe that every setback is moving them towards achieving the great success that is inevitable for them.

They believe in three Cs that are non-negotiable in the journey of reaching one's goals. Commitment, Completion and Closure.

Commitment: Great men and women are those who make clear, unequivocal commitments and then refuse to budge from them, no matter what happens. If commitment is ever seen as a casual virtue, you are heading towards disaster.

Completion: Quite often people don't complete a task giving it the same priority and intensity as when they started the job. This often results in the delay of final completion. Completing the task only up to the 90% or 95% level does not help the cause. Discipline to resist this natural tendency to delay and push completion is a sign of a successful person. The start and close of the task with same intensity is the key differentiator.

Closure: Bringing closure to an issue is absolutely essential for you to feel happy and in control. Lack of closure, unfinished business and incomplete action are major sources of stress, dissatisfaction and even failure. Have you heard the question, "How do you eat an elephant?" And the answer is, "One bite at a time."

One of the most important breakthroughs in thinking was explained by Elihu Goldratt in his book *The Goal* as "The Theory of Constraints." This theory says that between you and anything you want to accomplish, there is a constraint that determines how fast you get to where you want to go. For example, if you are driving down the freeway and there is traffic that is narrowing all the cars into a single lane, this bottleneck becomes the constraint that determines how fast you navigate to your destination.

Ask yourself, "What is it in me that is holding me back?" Is it your personality, temperament, skills, abilities, habits, education or experience? The primary obstacles between you and your goals are usually mental. And it is with these mental obstacles that you must first resign and make a fresh beginning if you want to achieve everything that is possible for you.

The two major obstacles to success and achievement are fear and doubt. As soon as you think of the goal, these fears overwhelm you and like a bucket of water on a small fire, they extinguish your desire completely. These fears and doubts arise out of ignorance and feelings of inadequacy. The more you learn the things you need to know to achieve your goals, the less fear you will feel, and the more courageous and confident you will become.

Be All You Can Be. The Market only pays excellent rewards for excellent performance. One of the qualities of top people is that, at a certain point in their careers, they decided to "Commit to Excellence." They decided to be the best at what they do. Les Brown, the motivational speaker says, "To achieve something that you have never achieved before, you must become someone that you have never been before." The very best way to develop yourself in the direction of your natural talents and interests is by adopting the principle of "Nurture your nature." This is extremely important advice that you should follow throughout your career.

As rightly said by Tom Hopkins, "Goals are the fuel in the furnace of achievement."

In the concluding session, you can take a look at these twenty-one steps for setting and achieving goals.

1. Unlock Your Potential – Always remember that your true potential is unlimited.
2. Take Charge of Your Life – You are completely responsible for everything you are today, for everything you think, say and do, and for everything you become.
3. Create Your Own Future – Imagine that you have no limitations. Think as if you had all the resources you needed to create any life that you desire.
4. Clarify Your Values – Your innermost values and convictions define you as a person. Refuse to deviate from what you feel is right for you.
5. Determine Your True Goals – Decide what you really want. Clarity is essential for happiness and high performance living.

6. Decide Upon Your Major Definite Purpose – You need a central purpose to build your life. Decide what it is for you and work on it all the time.

7. Analyze Your Beliefs – Make sure that your beliefs are positive and consistent with achieving everything that is possible for you.

8. Start At The Beginning – Do a careful analysis. Be both honest and realistic about what you want to accomplish in the future.

9. Measure Your Progress – Set clear benchmarks & measures. They help you to assess how well you are doing and enable you to make necessary adjustments and corrections.

10. Remove The Roadblocks – Problem solving is a skill you can master with practice.

11. Become An Expert In Your Field – Set this as a goal, work on it every day, and never stop working at it until you get there.

12. Associate With The Right People –Fly with the eagles if you want to be an eagle yourself.

13. Make A Plan Of Action – Your ability to plan and organize will enable you to accomplish even the biggest and most complex goals.

14. Manage Your Time Well – Always set priorities before you begin, and then concentrate on the most valuable use of your time.

15. Review Your Goals Daily – Make sure that you are still on track and that you are still working towards things that are important to you.

16. Visualize Your Goals Continually – Repeatedly "see" your goals as if they already existed. Your clear, exciting

mental images activate all your mental powers and attract your goals into your life.

17. Activate Your Superconscious Mind – Take the time regularly to tap into this amazing source of ideas and insights for goal attainment.

18. Remain Flexible At All Times – Be open to new, better, faster, cheaper ways to achieve the result.

19. Unlock Your Inborn Creativity –You are a potential genius, use it.

20. Do Something Every Day – Use the "Momentum Principle of Success." Action orientation is essential to your success.

21. Persist Until You Succeed – Persistence is self-discipline in action, and is the true measure of your belief in yourself.

Michael Jordan said, "Everybody has talent, but ability takes hard work." And most self-made millionaires say, "I never worked a day in my life." What they did was to find out what they really enjoyed, and then they did more and more of it.

02

Aligned Thinking

About the Author
(Jim Steffen)

Dr. R. James (Jim) Steffen, president and founder of Steffen, Steffen & Associates Inc. (SSA International), is an internationally known author, speaker, consultant and trainer. He is recognized as an expert in Aligned Thinking, Time Mastery, Leadership, Productivity and Successful Partnership, which focuses on very satisfied, loyal customers and employees.

He has worked with more than 160 Fortune 500 companies. Dr. Steffen has developed industry's most powerful tool Aligned Thinking Process, aligning every action towards what you really want.

Jim is a storyteller from beginning to end. He has more than thirty years of success stories to share and is an award-winning presenter.

Aligned Thinking, Published by Berrett-Koehler Publishers; 2006

Aligned Thinking

After spending nearly three fourth of your productive time at work you still have these questions that make you feel miserable. What have I really accomplished today? Why are there so many interruptions? It is quite true that routines create a lot of distractions. Whether we notice this or not, they are the main contributors to our growing frustration.

What would you do and how do you overcome these obstacles? One thing is definite; you need to change something when life is too long on work and too short on real meaning.

Aligned thinking offers insights to our daily struggle with work-life balance. It is everybody's story whether in the corporates or being an entrepreneur yourself. The industry hardly matters when the problems are universal.

The journey of becoming an Aligned Thinker depends on a set of tools that will help you discover the MIN Secret. What's the MIN Secret? MIN stands for **Most Important Now.**

It's an amazing concept that can be used by anyone. It is applicable to all; be it homemakers, students, entrepreneurs or academicians. It will help you achieve what you aim for. It will make you accountable, and when that realization happens, there is no looking back.

"You become an Aligned Thinker when what you really want from life and work drives every action, and every action takes you, step-by-step, back to what you really want."

MIN Secret is more valuable to people if they discover it themselves, as they experience the answers to the three most important questions.

MIN formula is explained by the three fundamental questions that affects all of us during our life time. We can align our life and thinking if we closely understand and follow these questions.

It is the Secret to your living as an Aligned Thinker.

- Purpose Question
- Focus Question
- Now Question

When you understand how to answer these three questions and live the answers, you'll discover the "Most Important Now" Secret.

Let's understand the process with the help of an example. When you learn to ride a bike, you master three things—steering, pedaling, and balancing. When you start, you don't necessarily try all these in one go. If you try all three you will probably fall, and continue to fall every time you attempt the same method.

However, if you try to learn the art of riding the bike, one step at a time, it will help you learn better and faster. If you just focus on guide first and let someone else balance and move you, it's easier. Then you attempt with the pedaling skill and finally pay attention to the balancing act.

When you get all three synchronized, you will have mastered the skill, and thereafter you will never forget how to ride a bike. Once you have got the basics right, you will never forget the art. You might be rusty if you don't ride the bike for some time, but whenever you decide to ride, you can pick it up quickly.

The three questions of Aligned Thinking and using the "Most Important Now" Secret are the same as learning to ride the bike. Once you get it, you will never forget it.

The Purpose Question

What do I really want from life and work?

The meaning of our daily actions comes from the purpose we assign to our life, to our goals. The most significant reason why we struggle for the search of this meaning is the non-alignment between our daily actions and what we want from our life or work. Putting in long working hours, our commitment to work only makes matters worse. Unfortunately, this non-congruence between work, commitment and what we want is the cause of problems for most of the people.

Aligned Thinking offers a three-step method to clarify the purpose question:

Step 1: Capture your values, desires and needs.

From the list of values, desires and needs, listed below, if you could have just one item, what would it be?

- Appreciation of arts
- Career
- Contribution to humanity
- Entertainment
- Family
- Financial well-being
- Friends
- Home
- Intellectual well-being
- Person I want to be
- Physical well-being
- Retirement
- Serving others
- Spiritual well-being
- Spouse/significant other
- Travel
- Any other_____

Step 2: Create your prioritized personal purpose.

A. Related to this one item, what do you want and why? Write your answer.
B. If you could have just one more item, what would it be? Circle it, then repeat A.
C. Repeat A and B until you have exhausted what you really want. Remember the catch, the more items you want,

the more difficult it is to focus on one. At the end of this exercise, you will have enough clarity with regard to the purpose.

Step 3: Review your purpose daily; refine it quarterly.

Plain reviewing will become a mundane job and kill the excitement. Instead create a fun day for purpose—for example, organize this meeting in some nice place that will pep up your mood and try repeating this each quarter just so to refine your purpose. Let this be the most awaited day of the quarter and let it be the most celebrated day to remember.

The next big thing that affects every individual which the author tries to explain is "how to keep yourself free of stress." Whenever you wish to be stress-free, you must begin your efforts from identifying the 'P' – Primary Desire, followed by 'NC' – Necessary conditions. Necessary Conditions are those conditions which are undoubtedly required to achieve Primary Desire. More often you will have the struggle dealing with the NCs and you will argue whether it is required or not. If you alter your attitude towards the NCs, they are definitely going to reward you in achieving your Primary Desire. To have fun with your NCs you need to make an attitudinal shift. Unless you see merit in your P, you will not be motivated to perform your NCs, but once you are in love with your P, you will have fun with your NCs.

The Focus Question

With the many options I have, how do I stay focused on what I really want?

The answer to this question is one of the easiest and most powerful Aligned Thinking tools I know. We commit five very common mistakes knowingly or unknowingly. Simple yet powerful skills are explained below, that will help you overcome them:

1. Not giving yourself a regular focus: Set aside 1 hour a week as a focused hour.

2. Not reviewing your professional and personal life purpose daily: The people who are successful in getting what they really want keep this question uppermost in their mind. If you don't review what you really want regularly, it's hard to see how your true purpose will motivate your every action.

3. Convert your to-do list to priority list: You'll get a triple benefit. You'll achieve more, achieve more of the important things, and feel more satisfied.

4. Not including personal priorities, like time for each other: When you set your priorities for the day or week to come, be sure to include several personal priorities along with business priorities.

5. Guesstimate how long each priority will take and adjust your plans accordingly.

The Now Question

Our life is like a huge pyramid and the only thing we control is the point at the top, which is the "now". Not knowing where to start is most people's dilemma. The very reason why they don't make every moment count is simply because they just don't stay focused on their now moment. They pay little attention to what they control and what they don't. Knowing exactly the difference between what you do and don't control will show you where to start. We can only control what we do in the present. Only I choose to be free and not a victim.

How do I get the most from the only thing I control—my actions now? The question will be easier to answer if we break it into three smaller questions, what, why, and how.

- What do I want to do now to get the most from this action?
- Why do I want to do this now?
- How do I want to do this action now to get the most from it?

When you are consistently involved in your Most Important Now, you're making every moment count.

Why is Most Important Now Secret called a secret? When you understand the Most Important Now idea, you just have to admit its powerful elegance.

Why call it a secret?

There are two primary reasons. First, most people don't understand it, so in some sense the elegance and power of the MIN question always remains secret to them.

Second, you have to understand its deeper meaning. You need to experience the answers to the purpose, focus and now questions and have the freedom attitude to truly understand the MIN Secret and make it work for you.

03

Work Reimagined

About the Author
(Richard J. Leider/David A. Shapiro)

For more than four decades, Richard has pioneered the way we answered the question, "Why do you get up in the morning?" As the founder of Inventure – the Purpose Company, he is ranked by Forbes Magazine as one of the "Top 5" most respected executive coaches in America and by the Conference Board as a "legend in coaching". Richard has authored ten books selling over one million copies.

He holds a master's degree in Counselling and is a National Certified Career Counsellor and a National Certified Master Career Counsellor. His works have been recognized with awards from the Bush Foundation and the Fielding Institute's Outstanding Scholar for Creative Longevity.

David A. Shapiro is a writer, consultant, and educator specializing in progressive business and personal development programs. A full-time faculty member at Cascadia College, Washington and Education Director of the University of Washington for Philosophy for Children, a non-profit organization that brings philosophy into the lives of young people in schools and community groups through literature, philosophical works, and classroom activities, David is an educator by heart.

His professional writer career began as a script writer for stand-up comedians, eventually getting him into writing corporate training material.

David is the author of *Choosing the Right Thing to Do* and has co-authored six more books.

Work Reimagined, Published by Berrett-Koehler Publishers; 2015

Work Reimagined

Work reimagined is a great read for people who would like to have insights and perspectives about self and would like to define and re-define work, purpose, passion and values in their professional lives.

The book throws on to us very interesting questions that we regularly use in our conversations with the outside world. What if we objectively pose the same question to ourselves? Can we honestly introspect and look for answers?

It may be the most common question we ask of others and which others ask of us. It is certainly one of the most important questions we can ask of ourselves:

- What do I do?
- What do I really do?
- What is my real work?

At a fundamental level, we all have the need to feel like "somebody," to do something that gives our life meaning and purpose, some reason to get up in the morning.

Work is important and responsible for our well-being. It is how we spend our time and what work we do ultimately is the deciding factor on how complete we feel about the whole thing. It is therefore very important that we find fulfilling work. Not surprisingly, it is one of the dominant aspirations of people everywhere, at all ages and phases of life.

It is though observed, contradictory to our need for fulfilment that we limit ourselves by doing what we think we should do.

But the fact remains that by doing what we love to, we expand our potential and increase the likelihood that the work that we do will be consistent with our gifts. We maximize our chances for creating a happy environment around us. We run to work and walk back home feeling contended and happy and with a sense of accomplishment.

Nobody but you know what work you should take up that will keep you happy. Maybe it means taking a job as a taxi driver. Perhaps it is to go to the seminary or teach philosophy to children. Maybe expressing your calling means to form a collectively owned organic farm or maybe it is to run for mayor of your small town. Or perhaps you will heed your calling to become a chef, a poet or teacher. There are thousands of callings and limitless ways to express them—and only we can name our calling and act upon it.

People who feel complete and fulfilled in their work tend to have exercised choice in getting where they are. They usually have, at some point or another, taken the proverbial "bull by the horns" and set a direction for their lives. They tend to have pursued that direction. They use their intuition as a compass to navigate through the ups and downs and make it to their destination. It is quite possible, during the journey, they may change course many times, but the mere fact of choosing their life's course enables them to purposefully pursue their dreams. And the sense of power that comes from knowing that their direction is freely chosen is immense and unexplainable.

The Napkin Test

Grab a piece of paper napkin and write down the simple formula: G + P + V = C, where "G" stands for Gifts, "P" stands for "Passion," "V" stands for "Values," and "C" stands for Calling. It is a profound formula, responsible for delivering the desired results.

Gifts + Passions + Values = Calling. It is really that simple. Uncovering our calling means identifying our gifts, applying them in support of something we are passionate about, in an environment that is consistent with our values. That, in essence, is what reimagining work is all about. A good job, career or calling blends all three together.

To get a better sense of your own passions, ask yourself: What keeps me up at night? What do I think is worth doing with my time? What do I obsess about? What challenges do I think need solving? What am I constantly reading about and talking to people about?

How would you define work? When you discover the inner satisfaction about doing something that you really care about, by utilizing your gifted talent. What is important to remember, though, is that this "something" need not be a big idea or exceptional effort or going out of your way or any do or die situation. It can be something much smaller, simpler but with cleaner intent, and by doing that work, it gives us the feeling of immense worth. It does not even have to involve the best aspects of people's lives; a perfectly satisfying—and meaningful—life can be derived from dealing on a daily basis with what most people choose not to deal with.

What inspires you? Something that consistently intrigues you makes you excited to explore, gives you energy and leads you to action. In other words, something that becomes a reason for you to look ahead in your life. Something that does not let you sleep and something that becomes a reason for your getting up in the morning

The answer to these questions provides insights into our passions. But how do we find passion in work? How do we achieve a connectedness to broader concerns? How do we commit to something larger than ourselves such that we feel an overwhelming sense of aliveness and purpose? All these questions take us into deeper conversation with self. It is a way to make an attempt to align our passion, purpose, thoughts and actions.

We express our values through the choices we make. Consequently, if we are living in a manner that is consistent with our values, our values will be apparent in the way that we live. The environment in which we work will reflect the kinds of things we care about. The way we spend our time and money, the friendships we cultivate and the relations we nurture are other ways we make our values apparent in the world.

In fact, many of us at one time or another have made choices that are decidedly at odds with our values. Many of us have found ourselves in situations that prevent us from being who we really are. The pressure to do well—that is, make money—gets in the way of our desire to do good. When that happens, we tend to lose sight of the very values that could enable us to find ourselves. We end up in a self-reinforcing system that drags us farther away from our values, farther away from ourselves. Eventually we end up losing ourselves.

Think of times in your own life when you have acted upon your values. Recall how it felt to stand up for a cause you believe in, even if it meant short-term hardship. Remember the sense of satisfaction that came from feeling connected to an idea or cause larger than yourself. There may have been financial implications; you may have had to sacrifice monetary success for successful expression of your values, but it was probably worth it. These are the experiences that make life worth living, the experiences that give meaning and purpose to our days. These experiences give us the courage to do something bigger and better with our lives.

To have such experiences more consistently, we have to do two things:

- We have to develop a deeper understanding of what our values really are
- We have to begin to act in ways that express those values in our daily lives.

Think of integrity, friendship, freedom, respect, as some values. Ask yourself which you value most highly. Which of those mentioned—or which others—would you list as your true values?

Then examine your answers more carefully to see if you have identified values you really do value.

The answers to questions like these reveal our legacy — our footprint, the music that plays after we are gone. When we explore our legacy we ask, "What do we want our lives to have been about?"

Our legacy emerges from a life that is lived with a purpose; we leave a legacy that is meaningful and makes a positive difference to our loved ones and us.

Always ask yourself, "Is there something larger than my own life that I care about?"

Many people die with their songs unsung, either due to lack of time, lack of clarity or lack of confidence. Then there are unexpected responsibilities, illnesses or changes in family situations, but the most common reason is *that they never really could identify their song.* However, it takes many years to understand and discover our own music because it requires discipline, and when it does come, it gives us deep satisfaction and pride.

We leave a legacy no matter what we do. The choices we made define the person we were whether we like it or not. It is just that some people leave legacies that express their true selves, while others simply leave an unfinished tune that signifies little of what they were really about.

As we reimagine work and our relationship to it, we benefit from considering how we can let our music be heard while we live, so it can continue to play even when we are no more.

When we uncover our inner urge, we feel free to bring our values to work, to take a stand for what we believe, to be the same person on the job as we are away from it.

In the end, what really matters, anyway? We are born, we live, we die; a thousand years from now, it is highly unlikely that any of us will be remembered. A million years from now, it is probable that the entire human race will be forgotten.

In spite of this, though, most of us feel like our lives matter. We generally think it makes a difference whether we do one thing or another. The choices that present themselves to us seem like real choices. Even though they might not affect our distant ancestors many centuries in the future, they do affect us and those around us. Our happiness, our satisfactions, our concerns—small as they are in the "such is life" scheme of things—fill up the universe from our perspective.

Life Is Beautiful. We make it passionate by giving it a purpose. True meaning of our life is served when we are committed to something that is larger than us. When we are absorbed in something larger than our own lives is when we feel most alive.

04

Courage Goes to Work

About the Author
(Bill Treasurer)

Bill Treasurer is a speaker, author and Chief Encouragement Officer of Giant Leap Consulting. Since the last two decades, his talks on courage, leadership and career backbone have benefited numerous people.

His insights on risk-taking and courage have been featured in over 100 newspapers and magazines.

Author of six books, Bill holds a master's degree from the University of Wisconsin and a bachelor's degree from West Virginia University where he attended school on a full athletic scholarship. He is a former U.S. High Diving Team captain and a cancer survivor.

Courage Goes To Work, Published by Berrett-Koehler Publishers; 2019

Courage Goes to Work

Courage is, most often, a behavioral response to a challenge. You see courage working when people trust your decisions instead of silently resisting your every move. Courage is working when employees raise the red flag on projects that need attention; it is working when people are candid and not nodding their heads to "yes" every time you talk. When people are full of courage, they're much more likely to TRY new things, TRUST you more fully, and TELL the truth more candidly.

People won't start being courageous just because you tell them to. You've got to create an environment that encourages them to extend themselves and take chances. In this section, you'll be introduced to four actions you need to take before expecting people to be more courageous. These four actions follow a specific order.

- The first action deals with role modeling, leading from the front.
- The second action deals with creating safety, providing support.

- The third action is putting fear to work. Fear has energy, which, if properly harnessed, can help to accomplish and overcome the very thing that causes fear.
- The fourth action deals with adjusting the degree of comfort and discomfort that employees experience.

Dustin Webster

Dustin Webster was a member of the U.S. High Diving team, a go getter, optimistic, undeterred and unfazed by rough weather. Before coming up to complex diving, Dustin had confronted plenty of other work challenges. Dustin practiced take-offs from the pool deck, then from the perch and later with further increase in height by twenty more feet. The process involved purposely moving from comfort to discomfort and back again. Each time Dustin got comfortable, he moved up.

Dustin Webster would go on to become a seven-time world cliff diving champion. High dives come in many forms, including skill-stretching jobs, big consequential assignments. Similar to Dustin, when employees face such challenges, confidently and courageously, a positive outcome is definite.

Beyond Fear

Fear creates the culture of suspicions. It lowers the morale, damages relationships, erodes trust and builds resentment. But fear is also an invitation to experience your own courage. Whenever you operate out of courage, you feel good about yourself. Employees get pumped with pride when they overcome things that are hard, challenging and scary. When you build people's courage, you also stretch their capabilities and boost their performance. So, when they experience the value of being courageous, they respond to work challenges with clarity, confidence and conviction.

You can build courage in individuals only if you encourage them to dominate their fears. When they dominate their fears they become more change embracing, loyal, committed, fearless and optimistic. When the perception of "mistake" is viewed from the learning point, you experience a workplace with trust and good intentions, making your company courageous.

Leading from the Front

Usually there are two ways to get things done: push from behind or attracting from the front. Leading from the front gives you a better understanding about the risks you're exposing them to and the courage required to meet the challenges. It also earns you a lot of credibility and respect. They hold the highest respect for managers who themselves do the uncomfortable things first before asking others to do them. Jumping First principle helps you understand your role as leader. If you want your team members to show more initiative, have more accountability, be more positive, then you must demonstrate these things first. Nothing is more powerful than role modeling the courageous behavior.

Safety Nets

People take risks depending on how safe they feel. Therefore, supporting their courageous actions will help them to take adequate risks. It isn't about reduced risk of failure or less work. It's about organization showing faith and confidence in the individual. If your aim is to help people to be more courageous, you'd be wise to create safety nets. For some, safety means financial stability, for others it's about their reputation. Individuals will never want to jeopardize their position by taking undue risk. As a leader, clear understanding of their concern will help you to craft each person's net. There are three specific ways of building safety nets regardless of which kind of safety is involved:

- Give people permission to be courageous.
- Value forward-falling mistakes.
- Provide air cover.

Giving Permission to Be Courageous

You can provoke courageous behavior by allowing them to be courageous. Permission enhances safety. By giving them your full presence, you'll cause them to feel valued and "allowed" to bring their fears out in the open.

Valuing "Forward-Falling" Mistakes

Clarify to employees the difference between good mistakes (best effort, bad results) and bad mistakes (sloppiness or lack of effort). Not all mistakes are equal, and wise managers know that not making any mistakes is just as dangerous as making too many. As long as the mistakes aren't habitual, and if they drive us into learning something new, then they're worth making.

When the focus is not on punishing or embarrassing but on the lessons learned then it goes a long way in creating a higher standard of professionalism. By allowing them to make their own mistakes you create a safety net that allows them to be more experimental and innovative.

Middle management is a tough place to be, because you're pulled at one end by the demands of your bosses and at the other by the needs of your direct reports. When you spend unreasonably more time with your boss or when you cut off your team member mid-sentence, they will soon start losing confidence in you and stop respecting you. But if you back your employees and provide them the support they need, they will appear to be more courageous. They want to feel that they matter, and that their needs are considered. It is easier for workers to be courageous when you create safety nets. Increased safety lessens fear and increases willingness to carry out uncomfortable tasks.

Three Ways to Harness Fear

How about Caging the Tiger?

A protective frame is like a cage you can build to contain your fear. As you strengthen your protective frame, you become capable of withstanding greater amounts of fear. It's like getting mentored by someone who has faced similar challenges and acquiring the skills you'll need to face the task.

How boring it would be to go to a zoo and see an empty cage. But if you spot the tiger outside its cage, either you'd freeze or run for your life. And the same fear will turn into excitement when you put the tiger (fear) back in the strong cage (protective frame). This protective frame builds confidence and capabilities to the tiger's intensity. Protective frames allow workers to harness and transform their fear.

Fear is experienced as displeasure, and excitement is experienced as pleasure. But the key is pleasurable or dis-pleasurable isn't determined by the situation, it's determined by the strength of the cage. A person who is well prepared will take challenges more positively than someone who isn't. This readiness helps him build a protective frame to convert fear into excitement.

Normalizing Fear

While dealing with fearful employees, we often tell them, "Don't be afraid," but mostly it is ineffective. So why not acknowledge that instead, because then fear becomes more ordinary, less of shame. Once you start to see fear as a normal part of workplace experience, you pay less attention, which allows you to shift the focus away from it.

Tie Fear to Courage

You can't be courageous unless you are afraid. When fear is included in the definition of courage, fearful situations turn into opportunities. People who stick on despite being fearful epitomize what it means to be courageous. This is exactly the type of behavior that you want to acknowledge and reinforce. Great careers are defined by courageous moments. The best evidence is when someone risks their job by giving feedback, politely but bluntly, that nobody else has the guts to give.

Use Fear's Energy

The best way to deal with fear is to use it against itself. When properly harnessed, it can provide momentum for facing challenging situations. Fear comes with challenge. You get sweaty palms by moving outside of your comfort zone and moving into your courage zone. It's inside your courage zone where the learning and growing happens.

Comfort Lowers the Standard

Comfort is a place where lethargy replaces energy, avoidance replaces initiative, and apathy replaces passion. Everything slows down and gets pushed off to the next day. The problem with comfort is that when it settles in for too long, it lowers the standards. It starts showing up in every aspect of your personality, right from attention to ambition. We talk about performing better within our zone of comfort, but if we become too comfortable, our skills start deteriorating. It is important to note that the more discomfort that comfort causes, the more likely we are to change and, potentially, grow.

When employees are in comfort zone, your role is to provide them with challenges that move them into a zone of discomfort. When they become too uncomfortable, bring them back to a place of confidence. This modulation between comfort and discomfort is the process to stretch their capacity for doing harder tasks. Each time you expose people to greater levels of discomfort and each time you intensify the challenges they face, you are, de facto, causing them to be more courageous.

To modulate means to vary the frequency or volume of a thing. With that in mind, here are three ways of modulating comfort:

- Answer the Holy Question.
- Provide energy-creating challenges.
- Practice lead-ups.

Answer the Holy Question

It only takes one basic question to understand the career aspirations of your workers. "What do you want?" Because when you know what people want, you are in a far better position to match their aspirations to the company's goals. And when goals are aligned, people pursue them with the same dedication and passion. It's easier to get people to perform courageous (and uncomfortable) tasks when those tasks tie in to the attainment of their personal goals.

Provide Energy-Creating Challenges

Few things generate as much positive energy as a worthwhile challenge. When John F. Kennedy set forth the challenge of landing a man on the moon by the end of the 1960s, he explained, "We choose to go to the moon in this decade and do the other things, not because they are easy, but because they are hard, because that goal will serve to organize and measure the best of our energies and skills, because that challenge is one that we are willing to accept, one we are not unwilling to postpone, and one which we intend to win...." The word passion means energetic dedication and willingness to suffer.

Practice Lead-Ups

Modulating comfort is a better approach because it allows you to give them incrementally more difficult challenges that groom their skills in a measured way. In the sport of diving this process is called "lead-ups." Lead-ups are the building blocks of complex assignments that enhance the level of preparedness. If you bypass you lower the chances of being successful.

Using lead-ups to modulate comfort helps get workers to do uncomfortable things, and with each lead-up, the employee is exercising more courage.

Courageous Behavior

Like all behaviors, courage can be developed, encouraged, and reinforced. When you become familiar with courageous behavior, you gain a deeper understanding of how to tap into and strengthen your own courage and the courage of those around you.

Courage Can Be Classified into Three Forms.

TRY Courage: When people make a first attempt, volunteering, venturing into a new area, they are exhibiting courage of initiative and action.

TRUST Courage: Not questioning the motive or intention and giving them the benefit of doubt is what TRUST Courage is all about.

TELL Courage: Encouraging individuals to speak up tactfully but truthfully, be it giving feedback or accepting their mistakes is Tell Courage.

Using the **TRY, TRUST, TELL** framework allows us to discriminate the different ways we have been courageous in the past and are capable of being in the future.

Courage and Fear – Two sides of the same coin

People are not either courageous or cowardly. They are both. Sometimes they stand for something important but sometimes they surrender meekly. It is these sets of actions and behaviors that determine whether they are courageous or fearful. These two management dispositions are called as Fillers and Spillers. When your bucket is filled with courage, you see the world with confidence. But when it is filled with fear, you see it as a threat. Because most managers are both Fillers and Spillers.

Good management starts with identifying three things:

1. Knowing which bucket you're operating out of
2. Discerning which bucket your employees are operating out of
3. Filling your bucket and their buckets with courage

You are a Filler manager when you build up people's confidence by encouraging them to face challenges. Your own successes are proof that their successes are possible. You are a Filler manager when your optimism about the future leaves people feeling more confident about themselves and more energized to deal with whatever challenges they are facing.

You are a Spiller manager when you undermine people's confidence. As a Spiller, you drain whatever courage people have. You are a Spiller manager when your pessimism leaves people feeling discouraged and less confident about themselves and the future.

A Filler manager assumes the best in people, encourages risk-taking and mistake making, views the future with optimism and makes people feel more confident and courageous. Spiller managers do the opposite.

TRY Courage

TRY Courage involves accepting challenges that you have never faced before. A new market entry can have a dramatic impact on the entire business. Beyond investing money, good reputation, solid networking and loyal customers, there is no guarantee that you'll be able to outshine the competition. So the risks are very high, which makes such ventures ripe for *TRY Courage*. It is only through trying relentlessly, persistently and awkwardly that courage will precede success. Filling people with *TRY Courage* involves helping them to attempt new things, take on messy problems that others avoid and persist in the face of setbacks. All of these, on some level, involve action and leadership.

TRUST Courage

TRUST Courage, for managers, is a tricky thing. When you trust, you become vulnerable to actions that are beyond your direct control. Your success becomes dependent upon someone else's action. Because of this risk, it takes courage to place trust in others. It takes *TRUST Courage* to let employees do their jobs without interference. For courageously trusting each other, we deepen our relationships and strengthen our communities. More important, TRUST Courage provides you with access to the best qualities that relationships have to offer, like friendship, support, joy and love.

TELL Courage

Regardless of how open a company considers itself to be, the risks of voicing an opinion that runs counter to the directives of the senior team are so high that most employees keep quiet. In the case of *TELL Courage,* the risk is in voicing your true opinion. You'll be set aside as an outcast from the established social order. The risk that comes with *TELL Courage* is the risk of social banishment.

The lack of *TELL Courage* demonstrated by employees is directly related to the behavior of managers. Specifically, when managers use intimidation to get things done, employees learn that speaking up is the best way to get thrown out. *TELL Courage* is the hardest to fill. There is often a decisive moment after someone asserts *TELL Courage.* In that moment what is told is the truth.

Making Choice

Courageous managers are sorely needed in the workplace. But becoming one means making a choice, and then committing yourself to living courageously, despite the constant pressures that comfort and fear present. What will your choice be?

When your behaviors are directed by courageous impulses, you are operating out of your best and braver self. "Problems" are increasingly viewed as opportunities and challenges. Courage refreshes, recharges, and recommits workers to their projects, teammates, and careers. In light of such benefits, the decision to pursue management by courage would seem obvious. But we both know that opting for courage means holding yourself to higher standards and ideals, which comes with its own set of challenges and realities. Here are some additional considerations to help you make an informed choice:

Be Careful What You Wish For: When employees are more courageous, they won't sit in their cubicles taking orders like well-trained circus animals. Courageous employees will press to take on more challenging roles. Courageous employees will voice their opinions and objections more freely. Courageous employees will challenge, aspire, risk, think, and lead.

You'll Need More Than Courage: Courage without brains is like ethics without a soul. There's smart courage and there's stupid courage. Courage, like power, leadership, and ambition, can be a misused means to an immoral end. Courage takes its fullest and noblest form when it is shaped and tempered by intelligence, discipline, focus, and morality.

Get Ready to Enter Naysayer Territory: Just as often as courage wins admiration, it provokes anger and outrage. The courage that brings out the best in you or your employees may bring out the worst in others. Naysayers surround courageous people the way zombies surround the hero in a horror movie. For every ten naysayers there will be at least one powerful yeasayer cheering from the sidelines. Courage is inspirational and attractive.

A Moment of Courage Can Have an Enduring Career Impact: To live a fulfilling life, one has to be able to live within his or her own skin. One moment of courage can change the entire trajectory of your life. This courage stuff is serious business! When you decide to start your own business, or buck for a promotion, or quit your six-figure job to become a teacher, you're going to be a very different person in the long run. You and your courage are needed because you have the best chance of bringing positive change to the world of work.

Be Courageous!

Regrets, especially over things we should have done but didn't because we were too comfortable or afraid when we faced them, burn hot in our souls. The risks we regret the most re always the ones we didn't take.

Be Courageous! Whether it is asking for a raise or suffering career setback. Be Courageous when situations or people try to compromise your integrity. Be Courageous when you or someone else is being bullied. Be Courageous when you are deciding whether to start your own business. In work and in life, for yourself and for others, in all you do and say, Be Courageous!

Courage has been living inside you since the day you were born. You were courageous on your first day of school. You were courageous when you learned how to drive a car. You were courageous when you went on your first job interview, became a manager, and led a huge project for your company. You were courageous every time you were afraid and uncomfortable but carried on anyway. All you have to do now is more of what your whole life has been teaching you to do: Be Courageous!

05

Choosing the Right Thing to Do

About the Author
(David A. Shapiro)

David A. Shapiro is the Education Director of the Northwest Center for Philosophy for Children, a non-profit organization that brings philosophy into the lives of young people in schools and community groups. He is the author/co-author of six books.

Choosing the Right Thing to Do, Published by Berrett-Koehler Publishers; 1999

Choosing the Right Thing to Do

What Makes Right Acts Right, Good Things Good and Bad Things Bad?

Let's begin with an opinion on slavery. If someone says "slavery is wrong" it is only true to what it means to me because I think slavery is wrong. You might say, "slavery is just fine," and that's an equally valid opinion. Even though our views differ, they're both true; yours is just true for you, mine is true for me.

It only goes to say that we can take cognisance of other's views and judge them as wrong, but it will be inappropriate to react and get violent towards that opinion. It is wrong to physically hurt that person for holding on to his beliefs.

The same is true in our daily routine. We all at some point or other come to the crossroad of choosing a career or submitting to our family needs. Caring for children, parents, their daily routine and sacrificing our ambition for the sake of well-being of our family. While pursuing careers, we confront this situation and try to dodge the moral dilemma. Whether or not should we work longer hours to provide them with material advantages even though it means spending less time together? Or should we forego career opportunities to have more time with them. Although this means they won't have all that their friends have? To solve this dilemma, most of us will reason out in some way; we'll weigh the pros and cons and eventually come up with a decision. When our actions and thoughts are not in sync, our final decision turns out to be opposite of our reasoned decision. It's like flipping a coin to decide what to do, and when heads comes up we suddenly realize that what we really want to do is tails.

Examining the way a person resolves moral dilemmas provides insight into his or her decision-making process. And when it's our own process we're examining, the insight is even more telling.

When trying to figure out the right thing to do, people generally appeal to a variety of considerations that can be broken down as follows:

Feelings vs. Principles: Some people trust their moral sensibilities to tell them what to do while others use their heads more than their hearts.

Motives vs. Outcomes: Some people want to make sure that the reasons for a particular decision are morally praiseworthy, while others look at the consequences of their choice.

Individual vs. Societal Considerations: Some concentrate on the type of person they will become while others turn their attention to be accepted by the society they live in.

At the same time, most businesspeople are interested in doing the right thing only up to a particular point. It is when they are required to make a choice between conscience and competition that they tend to go with competition. Competition always weighs more over conscience, and then we justify our decision by telling ourselves that everyone does it. Do we ever think what kind of moral legacy we are leaving behind? Does such a decision talk about our business ethics? It just goes to say that the line is very thin, and it's the competition that mostly overtakes the conscience.

We don't live in a perfect world. It's perfectly obvious that good things do happen to bad businesspeople, and that there are plenty of not-so-nice businesspeople out there.

How you'd judge a car dealer who intentionally sold you a defective piece compared to the one who wasn't aware that the vehicle had problems. Therefore, the right thing is more than just a matter of knowing what it is.

We often face issues at the workplace related to "Integrity". As businesspeople, we often confront situations that call our integrity into question. Is there anything we can do about it? Can we set up a right example, by being a role model, by setting up high moral standards, to ensure that we leave a solid ethical legacy behind us? The manner in which we address things exemplifies the person we are trying to be.

Kant proposed the Golden Rule; it says that we should treat others as we would have them treat us. How true is this rule? Does it mean that if I am treated wrong, I should treat others wrong as well?

Twentieth-century social and political philosopher John Rawls proposed a theory to ensure fairness in the rules by which society is governed. According to Rawls, rules that count as fair are those that everyone would agree to if everyone could freely and impartially choose them.

Warren Buffett explained Rawls' theory in a speech he gave at the University of Washington. A student asked him how he would run things if he were in charge. Buffet continued, let's say it's 24 hours before you're going to be born, and a genie appears. And the genie says, "You look like a real winner, I'm going to let you set the rules of society: economic, political, social. And these rules are going to apply for your lifetime, and your children's lifetime, and grandchildren's." So you ask, "What's the catch?"

"The catch is, you don't know if you're going to be rich or poor, black or white, male or female.... So what rules do you want to have?"

Let's put up this in our workplace. Suppose you didn't know whether you were boss, subordinate, co-worker, client, supplier, a stockholder in your company, or a member of a community in which your company does business. What principles would you choose to guide people's behavior? How would you sketch out possible scenarios so that no matter what character in that scenario you happened to be, the result for you would be as good as possible?

But as Norman Bowie has pointed out in the idea of Reciprocal Obligation, the relationships among businesses and their stakeholders have to be two-way. If, as employees, we expect our employers to treat us fairly, with dignity and respect, then we need to fulfill our obligations to be loyal and trustworthy. Or if, as customers, we expect that businesses should "go the extra mile" for us, it's only fair that we should be willing to do the same for them as well.

Sometimes we get what we want by doing what we should. Then, we have every reason for doing the right thing. It's easy to convince ourselves to make the moral choice.

Let's understand morality with the example of "diet." It basically means person giving up on some type of food which otherwise was up for consumption. It is just another way to let others know that we are not eating certain food. Like "No cake for me, I'm dieting." The word "diet" has thus become synonymous with self-denial or self-control. Restricting oneself from craving food.

In the same context, there is another meaning of diet, that refers to what we do eat. To say, "I'm on a diet" is insignificant, irrelevant. We're always on a diet, we can't survive without diet. But my diet is the choice I make about what to eat. My diet isn't about self-denial, it's about choice.

Morality can be looked at in the same way. Most of the time the focus is on what's wrong. But it doesn't have to be this way. Morality isn't what restrains us, it's what leads us. Our systems of ethics don't steer us away from what's wrong, they point us toward what's right. We're not dieting when we choose to do the right thing; rather, our moral choices represent our steady diet of attitudes and behaviors that are most conducive to our long-term health.

Science-fiction writer Isaac Asimov wondered about it this way: "Is the only reason you are virtuous because that's your ticket to heaven? Is the only reason you don't beat your children to death because you don't want to go to hell? It seems to me that it's insulting to human beings to imply that only a system of rewards and punishments can keep you a decent human being. Isn't it conceivable that a person wants to be a decent human being because he feels better?"

Remember that the choices we make don't define us instantly. It's the cumulation of such acts together that defines our character. One wrong act doesn't make you a bad person, nor does one act of generosity make you wonderful.

We either fail or refuse to accept that our lives are bigger than what we imagine them to be. The choices we make have wide-ranging implications, and our moral legacy will remain long after we are gone.

Every choice we make goes into creating our moral legacy. None of us gets a special "get out of jail free" card when it comes to how we will be remembered. It is possible to hide the truth or to cover up embarrassing or shameful facts about ourselves. But that doesn't change the embarrassing or shameful fact of the matter, whether or not we admit it to anyone else or even ourselves. A story in which the character we are playing reflects our true character, in which the choices we make represent an authentic expression of our deepest values, in which our moral legacy really reflects how we would most like to be remembered.

In Mark Twain's *The Adventures of Tom Sawyer*, Tom, Huckleberry Finn, and Joe Harper enjoy an opportunity that none of us can reasonably look forward to. They get to attend their own funeral and hear the sermon preached in their remembrance. Twain describes what the boys, who are believed by their townspeople to have drowned in the Mississippi river, witness from their hiding place in the unused church gallery:

> *As the service proceeded, the clergyman drew such pictures of the graces, the winning ways, and the rare promise of the lost lads that every soul there, thinking he recognized these pictures, felt a pang in remembering that he had persistently blinded himself to them always before, and had as persistently seen only faults and flaws in the poor boys. The minister related many a touching incident in the lives of the departed, too, which illustrated their sweet, generous natures, and the people could easily see, now, how noble and beautiful those episodes were, and remembered with grief that at the time they occurred they had experienced such mischievous duds, well deserving of the whip. The congregation became more and more moved, as the pathetic tale went on, till at last the whole company broke down and joined the weeping mourners in a chorus of anguished sobs, the preacher himself giving way to his feelings, and crying in the pulpit.*

Who wouldn't give anything to have that same opportunity? Who wouldn't love to experience such an outpouring of affection from friends, family members and townspeople? Wouldn't most of us, like Tom, seriously consider faking our own demise in order to find out just how we were being remembered?

Our legacy naturally intrigues us. It's perfectly understandable that we would want to know how the world will recall us after we're gone. The question is: How many of us are living our lives so that our legacy will reflect all that we truly hold most near and dear? How many of us, in other words, are living our lives with integrity, where integrity is defined as being the same person you are when you're alone as you are when you're not?

Being a good person doesn't require that we always make the best choice. We can qualify as virtuous by consistently doing good things, even if they aren't necessarily unsurpassed in their excellence. It's important to keep in mind that being good doesn't entail being perfect. We don't have to beat ourselves up just because we're not saints. It's enough to aspire and to accomplish to be merely good human beings.

May we all have the wisdom to perceive and choose the right thing to do, and in doing so, leave a moral legacy that distinguishes our lives, our memories, and ourselves.

06

Collaborating with the Enemy

About the Author
(Adam Kahane)

Adam Kahane is the Director of Reos Partners, an international social enterprise that helps people move forward together on their most important and intractable issues.

Adam is the author of the book *Solving Tough Problems: An Open Way of Talking, Listening, and Creating New Realities*, about which Nelson Mandela said, "This breakthrough book addresses the central challenge of our time: finding a way to work together to solve the problems we have created."

Adam has a B.Sc. in Physics (First Class Honors) from McGill University (Montreal), an M.A. in Energy and Resource Economics from the University of California (Berkeley), and an M.A. in Applied Behavioral Science from Bastyr University (Seattle). He has also studied negotiation at Harvard Law School and cello performance at Institute Marguerite-Bourgeoys.

Collaborating with the Enemy, Published by Berrett-Koehler Publishers; 2017

Collaborating with the Enemy

Working with People You Don't Agree with or Like or Trust

Very often, at every phase of our life, we face the challenge of working with people either we don't like or trust. We find ourselves at the cross roads, where collaboration seems both imperative and impossible. At the same time resolving the dilemma of opposites when work is critical can be very stressful. What do we do?

Collaboration conventionally means that people coming together are on the same page and same direction. But when we are working in complex and dynamic situations, conventional collaborations aren't successful.

For complex problems we should look at unconventional collaboration techniques. Stretch collaborations is one of its kind; it abandons the assumption of control. It gives up unrealistic fantasies of harmony, certainty, and compliance, and embraces messy realities. Stretch collaboration is a difficult method but has the capacity to get things done even in complex situations, with diverse others.

Stretch collaboration recommends three fundamental shifts in our working pattern:

First, change in mindset, from focusing on goals and team harmony to rather embracing both conflict and connection within and beyond the team.

Second, avoid being rigid in our expectations about the problem, the solution, and the plan. We must attempt to move forward and experiment with different perspectives and possibilities.

Third, not to interfere and try to impose change. At the same time we must focus on getting into action and exhibiting willingness to change ourselves.

Why is Collaboration Necessary and Difficult?

Generally, people who are the cause of our problems, we consider them as rivals, competitors, opponents, enemies and so on. But there are other categories as well. For example, in couples, most people think the other partner has a problem. They try to convince themselves by thinking aloud hoping that counselling will make their partner understand the problem and help them change. This mindset reduces the space for solving the problem and only aggravates the issue.

Collaboration is therefore both necessary and difficult, be it personal or professional. The wider the difference in views, the more difficult to collaborate. The challenge is to work jointly with but also to cooperate unwillingly with the enemy.

This challenge becomes acute as things become uncertain, complex and ambiguous. But it is imperative to collaborate because we need them, and not collaborating is not an option. So, what do we do when we think it is necessary to work with these people? We see their values and behaviors as different from ours; we believe they are wrong or bad and we feel frustrated or angry. We worry that we will have to compromise because collaboration with those people is unavoidable. How can we succeed, then, in working with people we don't agree with?

Four Ways to Deal with Problematic Situations

- Collaboration
- Forcing
- Adapting
- Exiting

Many people think of collaboration as the option, but that isn't true always. It is a choice; we all have to think whether or not to collaborate. We look for collaborating with others when we think we alone cannot do it. Collaboration brings in different perspectives and presents the opportunity to find a more effective way of finding impactful and sustained solution to the problem. It certainly brings the risk of compromising on our core values and the risk of betrayal, but it is still the preferred option to forcing, adapting and exiting.

Forcing for many people is the way to effect change. The risk is, we try to push through what we think is right and needs to be done. Others who think differently will push back, and therefore we will not achieve the desired outcome.

Adapting happens when we think that we cannot change our situation and so we need to find a way to live with it. We therefore ignore the situation and focus on moving on with life, fitting into what is happening around us.

Exiting is giving up. When we think we cannot change our situation and we are no longer willing to live with it. Sometimes exiting is simple and easy, and sometimes it requires us to give up a lot that matters to us.

From this perspective, we choose to combine collaboration and adapting when exiting and forcing is out of bounds. Put another way, we adapt or exit when others appear to be more powerful, alternately we apply force strategy when we are more powerful. Collaboration happens only when our power is evenly matched and neither of us can impose our will.

It is easy to begin to collaborate when we and the others all agree that we need to and want to. Others very often feel the pressure of collaborating with us. We must wait for their frustration and doubt to settle down. At the same time we must try to help them see the brighter side and increase their excitement, curiosity and hope by getting a third party to testify the authenticity of our intent. We then face the next question: How can we do this successfully?

Juan Manuel Santos – Story of Unconventional Stretch Collaboration

In 1996, a young politician named Juan Manuel Santos visited South Africa and met with Nelson Mandela, who told him about the Mont Fleur project. South Africa was at a stage, where people were ultimately left with two options. One, to get down on their knees and pray for a band of angels to come down from heaven and solve their problems for them or the second option was, that they worked things through together.

Looking into the merit of this approach, Santos developed some hope of getting Colombia out of the grip of civil war. He started organizing meetings involving generals, politicians, professors, and company presidents. In such an uncertain and complex time, the participants were both excited and nervous to find themselves in such a heterogeneous group.

Out of this meeting the collaborative project named Destino Colombia was initiated. The organizing committee consisted of military officers, guerrillas, and paramilitaries; activists and politicians; businesspeople and trade unionists; landowners and peasants; academics, journalists and young people.

As the work progressed, the team worked out four possible scenarios.

- The first was to just let things be and adapt to the situation that meant Colombia would further go into a state of chaos.
- The second scenario was to compromise between the government and the guerrillas, conventional collaborating.
- The third option was for the government to crush the guerrillas militarily and pacify the country, forcing their way.
- The fourth, "In Unity Lies Strength," to take along every participating member and exhibit mutual respect and cooperation. Although this was the most difficult scenario, it was still a possible option of stretch collaboration.

The team failed to agree on any particular solution, so they presented these scenarios to their fellow citizens through various mediums, as proposed possibilities.

In 2010, when Santos got elected as the President of the country, he characterized his government's program as an enactment of "In Unity Lies Strength." In 2016, Santos finally succeeded in negotiating a peace treaty with the FARC (Revolutionary Armed Forces of Colombia) and was awarded the Nobel Peace Prize. The Destino Colombia project brought an end to a fifty-two-year civil war.

Stretch collaboration is all about working with others, people we like or dislike and making our way. It is all about taking a first step, not knowing the route, but only to discover along the way. In stretch collaborations, participants come together voluntarily with no control on one another, always keeping the option of quitting open. The only sensible way to move forward is to take one step at a time and learn as we go.

Management professor Peter Senge says, "Most leadership strategies are doomed to failure from the outset. Leaders instigating change are often like gardeners standing over their plants, imploring them: 'Grow! Try harder! You can do it!' No gardener tries to convince a plant to 'want' to grow: if the seed does not have the potential to grow, there's nothing anyone can do to make a difference."

Stretch collaboration is like gardening. We can create some of the conditions for a collective effort to flourish, but we cannot direct it to do so. It is an ongoing process in which it is more important to act than to agree. What is crucial is to create the conducive environment for participants to act freely and creatively, working towards finding a workable solution. Success in collaborating does not mean to agree or like or trust, it simply means to remove the bottleneck and march ahead.

In stretch collaboration, we try out ideas that we think might work and then learn from the results. We articulate and test our assumptions, trying to discover errors early on, when they are smaller and easy to fix.

Creativity requires Negative Capability

The process of experimenting is a process of creating. We see Picasso willingly destroy his creation, because he is not concentrating on one aspect of his painting but the whole painting. The needed inner gestures here are fearlessness in letting go of what isn't working and boldness in proposing new solutions.

Working in this way requires being able to look at a still inadequate and still incomplete result without becoming frightened ("I am a failure!") or attached ("This must be right!"). We need to be present to what is actually happening rather than what we wish would happen. We need to be able to maintain our equanimity in a conflictual, uncomfortable situation where we don't know how things will turn out, or when, or even if we will succeed. The poet John Keats called this "negative capability," which he defined as "being capable of being in uncertainties, mysteries, and doubts without any irritable reaching after fact and reason."

One of the reasons why stretch collaboration is so daunting is that it requires us to undertake this kind of patient and relaxed experimentation and iteration—and to do so not only privately, like a painter or poet, but together with our opponents and enemies, on issues that really matter to us, risking having our mistakes exposed publicly.

Four Ways of Talking and Listening

The success of Stretch Collaboration heavily depends on the four modes of talking and listening skills of the individual.

Downloading – This type is exhibited typically by experts, dictators, and people who are either arrogant, angry or afraid. Such people do not listen to others because they think that their part of the story is the only truth. They are selective listeners, who will hear only what they want to listen to. People who don't agree with or like or trust one another always start in downloading mode ("The truth is...").

Debating – This is typically exhibited by judges. They focus on the objectivity and factual information of the matter ("This is correct and that is incorrect"). Here talking means challenging ideas where some people's ideas get accepted and some don't. This is a more open source of communication than downloading because people can express views and opinions and none of them is forcing the truth on the other ("In my opinion...").

Dialoguing – This is a self-reflective type of talking, more emphatic and subjective. This mode opens up new possibilities.

Presencing – This means the process of letting go of our ego, and letting in the awareness, deeper source of knowing. The individual or group starts with high energy levels and a sense of future possibility that is going to emerge.

All these modes are legitimate and useful. If we want to create possibilities and new realities, then we need to be able to spend at least some of our time dialoguing and presencing and not getting fixated at downloading and debating.

The third stretch is the biggest. If we want to get important things done in complex situations, then instead of blaming and watching others, we must shift our focus onto what we ourselves are doing: how we are contributing to things being the way they are and what we need to do differently to change the way things are.

We are co-creators, but there is a risk of becoming unbalanced if we start focusing on what others are doing. When we shift the focus on self we liberate ourselves and give ourselves direct opportunity to effect change. Instead of blaming others and pushing or cajoling or waiting for them to do their work, we can get on with our own.

Getting on with our own work requires us to see and acknowledge our own role and responsibility. Leadership scholar Bill Torbert once said, "If you're not part of the solution, you're part of the problem," but it misses a more important point, which is that if you are not part of the problem, then you cannot be part of the solution.

Stretch collaboration therefore requires that we see ourselves as part of the situation we are trying to address. I can phone home to say that I will be late "because I am in traffic" or "because I am traffic." The latter explanation explicitly opens up my options to work with others to change the situation.

The primary obstacle you will face in learning to stretch is overcoming the familiarity and comfort of your habitual way of doing things. You will need to bring in a change in your approach from being authoritative to accommodative. You will need to keep your options flexible and be open in your views and opinions: to sacrifice your smaller, constricted self to your larger, freer one. These stretches can therefore feel both frightening and liberating.

So in learning to collaborate, the people you think of as your enemies can, surprisingly, play a helpful role. Stretching requires you to move toward rather than away from different others. You will learn the most in those situations you find most difficult: when others do not do as you want them to and so force you to pause and find a fresh way forward.

Your enemies can be your greatest teachers.

07

Making the
Impossible Possible

About the Authors
(Kim Cameron/Marc Lavine)

Kim Cameron is a William Russell Kelly Professor of Management and Organizations at the University of Michigan and co-founder of the Center for Positive Organizational Scholarship.

His research work has been published in 130 academic articles and fifteen scholarly books. He is co-author, co-editor of fourteen books, including Developing Management Skills, Positive Organizational Scholarship, and Making the Impossible Possible.

Marc Lavine is a doctoral student and lecturer in the Department of Organization Studies at the Carroll School of Management at Boston College. He has consulted to multinational firms and non-profit organizations on issues of social responsibility, organizational learning, and strategic growth. *Making the Impossible Possible* is Mark's first book.

Making the Impossible Possible, Published by Berrett-Koehler Publishers; 2006

Making the Impossible Possible

Making the Impossible Possible is one of the finest demonstrations of execution excellence. It represents the story of unparalleled and unbelievable performance of the team involved in closure and cleaning up of the U.S. Government's nuclear weapon plant.

In March of 1951, the U.S. government's Atomic Energy Commission publicly reported that it would build a highly secure nuclear weapons plant on the eastern slope of the Rocky Mountains in Colorado. The U.S. felt the need to build its nuclear arsenal due to rising unrest with the Soviet Union. The site was labeled as Rocky Flats due to the nature of the place.

Rocky Flats was the most productive and efficient facility in the world until 1989. But later, due to environmental violations and rising health concerns, the FBI raided the facility and decided to close the site. In the year 1995, the U.S. government finally concluded to clean up and decommission the production facility.

Decision to close and clean up the facility posed numerous challenges:

It was the first of its kind, and no one in the industry knew how to clean up a plutonium production facility. With almost no or very little experience in nuclear clean up, it was too much of a risk.

Dealing with three different unions (steelworkers, building trades and security guards) with the growing unaddressed grievances was a major bottleneck.

Bringing a culture change all of a sudden from the life lived in secrecy, protection, and concealment to that of openness, transparency and futurism was exceedingly difficult.

Cleaning up one of the most polluted nuclear facilities in America with contamination all around including the soil and underground water was highly improbable.

Controlling and living through the public anger was challenging, because they knew that this facility was posing danger to surrounding communities.

Managing employees' aspirations when none anticipated the closure of the facility was difficult too. There was no meaningful work to keep them engaged. All their dreams were shattered and falling like a pack of cards. Fund allocation and the doubt on the competency of the contractor to successfully complete the clean-up was another challenge. Everybody was nervous and the stakes were very high.

Finally, after thorough competitive bidding process, the contract was awarded to Kaiser-Hill in 1995. It was initially for five years, and later was extended for another five years, after adding the cleaning up scope under a no-bid closure contract. A detailed report was submitted with the timeline of 70 years and spending of almost $36 billion. According to the DOE (Department of Energy) official it was gross underestimate of time and budget, and felt that the estimation of 200 years could have been more realistic.

What makes this story worth telling is that the entire project was completed 60 years early and at almost $30 billion savings. Other DOE clean-up projects in the United States with similar estimates of time frame and budget have not come close to the success achieved at Rocky Flats either in terms of time or budget.

Rocky Flats was closed and cleaned up, and was turned into a wildlife refuge. All structures were demolished, all surface waste was removed and soil and underground water were remediated to better than mandated standards. This project was completed at an estimated cost of $7 billion, including the expenditures in the years before Kaiser-Hill took over.

Alongside, there were improved relations with the three unions and grievances were reduced to a handful per year. More than 200 technological innovations were produced with faster and safer performance. *"Making the Impossible Possible"* represents performance that exceeded even the most optimistic estimates by a wide margin.

The story explains how this positively deviant performance occurred and the abundance approach that accounted for it.

The Abundance Approach

An abundance approach emphasis on good human conditions means not only doing well, but creating goodness that has a lasting effect. It works on the assumption of "embrace and enable our highest potential." It focuses on thriving outcomes and on virtuousness, and in contrast to a problem-solving approach.

The latter approach focuses on identifying and solving problems, addressing deficits and weaknesses, and overcoming challenges and obstacles. Contrary to the problem solving approach, the abundance approach focuses on closing the gaps between acceptable performance or even successful performance, and spectacular so-called virtuous performance.

Focusing on abundance gaps produces a heliotropic effect. In other words it unleashes positive potential leading to extraordinary performance.

Heliotropic effect is defined as a natural tendency of any living system to be inclined towards positive energy and staying away from the negative energy. It is evident within individuals and organizations in many ways, either physiologically, psychologically, emotionally, visually or socially.

Physiologically, for example, when a person believes that the medicine will be effective, then 60% of the time it will be effective, known as "placebo effect". If a teacher thinks students are bright then they are. This psychological effect is called as Pygmalion effect. It responds to our expectations and also of others' expectations. Similarly, the emotional effect can be seen within individuals with different mindsets. The one who is depressed, angry and pessimistic has low immunity as compared to the one who is happy, calm and positive. The heliotropic effect also occurs through positive energy. When exposed to positive people around us we tend to flourish.

The research shows that organizations that are high performing have three times more positive energizers than normal organizations. When an abundance approach is implemented in organizations, positive consequences are amplified, and they become self-reinforcing and at the same time it acts as a buffer towards any negativity.

The Role of Leaders

Most organizations attribute the change to a single leader's vision, strategy and charisma. However, in projects like Rocky Flats, successful leadership always emerges in multiple places and among multiple people. The success of the project of this magnitude does not go to any single leader. A clear message from the study of the Rocky Flats transformation: "No single person was the hero, but many were essential in making the project successful."

Leadership role at Rocky Flats was assigned to several individuals. Each was credited with articulating the vision and championing the idea that the closure and clean-up could be completed substantially faster and at a much lower cost than suggested.

The first important leadership role is idea champions. They are inspirational leaders who articulate a motivating vision and energize the team.

Second important type of leadership role is the sponsor role. They help acquire resources and support, and provide encouragement. They sponsor others' ideas, and without this sponsorship, effective change is impossible.

The third key leadership role is orchestrator. They orchestrate the vision and bring everyone together for implementation. They often cannot articulate, but they are the ones who make the vision or idea become a reality.

No significant large scale change will happen without all three leadership roles being performed, congruently with each other. And leaders need levers, enablers to produce extraordinary performance. To identify the key enablers, it is important to have a framework so that they can be organized. Rocky Flats chose to organize enablers in "Competing Values Framework."

Competing Values Framework

Competing Values Framework concept was developed to explain effective organizational performance. It highlights the functioning of high performing organizations with harmony and tensions. That is, excellence is always associated with the presence of tension, simultaneous opposites and paradox. By applying this concept it was easy to simplify leadership principles.

A study says, some organizations are effective when they demonstrate "flexibility and adaptability", while some had shown effectiveness working with "stability and control". There are organizations that were found effective, when they maintained "efficient internal process" and some were effective when they paid attention to "competitive external positioning".

Each of these four quadrants were identified based on their specific strengths and distinct characteristics.

- Collaborate
- Create
- Compete
- Control

Collaborate: Emphasizes building human capital, developing people, and strengthening the culture. Focus is on human development, human empowerment, and human commitment. Organizations succeed because they hire, develop, and retain their human resource base. Here effectiveness is associated with supportive interpersonal relationships, building cohesive teams and fostering engagement. Leaders in this quadrant produce working environments that are free of conflict and tension.

Create: Emphasizes creativity, agility, and constant change. The key is innovate, take risks, and envision the future. Organizations excel because they effectively handle discontinuity, change, and risk. Effectiveness is associated with entrepreneurship, innovation, vision, and constant change. They can predict the future and adapt to dynamic conditions. Leaders in this quadrant are visionaries and futurists, inclined toward risk, and unafraid of uncertainty.

Compete: Emphasizes aggression and force. Speed is an essential element in accomplishing goals and maintaining a competitive edge. The key here is compete hard, move fast, and play to win. Effectiveness is associated with aggressive action, fast response, and external customer focus. Leaders tend to be hard driving, direct, and competitive in this quadrant. They welcome challenges and stretch goals, and success is judged on the basis of results and not efforts.

Control: Emphasizes efficiency and carefully controlled processes. The mantra is to refine, reduce, and perfect. Effectiveness is associated with capable processes, measurement, and control and putting it to optimum use. Leaders in this quadrant pay attention to details and make careful decisions.

What is notable about the four quadrants is that they represent contradictory assumptions and competing values. The analysis helps uncover the paradoxical nature of excellence achieved at Rocky Flats. What is also key to understand is that "Enablers" are the factors that make change possible.

In explaining the spectacular success at Rocky Flats, four categories of enablers were identified:

A Clear, Shared Vision of the Future

The Rocky Flats project began with the reputation of a negative, depressing, doomed-to-failure project. It was all filled with negativity, criticism and cynicism. A clear, positive vision of the future was a prerequisite for making any progress at Rocky Flats. As a vision began to be formulated, it was not immediately accepted by all agencies. In order to make everyone believe, to look real and important, it was necessary to create the visual image that supported the vision. Clear vision resulted in alignment of multiple groups, and it made everyone believe that achieving something previously thought to be impossible was actually possible.

Symbolic Leadership Activities

The rationale for these symbolic activities was to make it clear to Rocky Flats employees that Rocky Flats was now in transition phase. The actual work of clean-up and closure was also marked as symbolic and meaningful. Destruction of buildings provided significant evidence of culture change.

Several actions were taken by Kaiser-Hill leaders to symbolically change the image of Rocky Flats' future and one was a name change. Sharing of profits earned from the fast-paced work with the workforce was an important symbolic announcement. What followed next was high level of commitment, cooperation and teamwork, and mutual respect across the group was reinforced.

Innovation and Creativity

The demands of this project made innovativeness a prerequisite for success. It was not the environmental conditions that led to dramatic success, but an orientation toward innovation. Kaiser-Hill approached the Rocky Flats project with an attitude of try it, find a way, and learn from mistakes. Being told "no" opened a door so that they could do something else that would be successful. One way in which innovation occurred was simply challenging existing rules and regulations that seemed to slow the process. Questioning red tape and bureaucracy was one of the most fruitful areas for confronting existing procedures and creating innovation. Kaiser-Hill's approach to innovation and experimentation wasn't always successful but every failure, and disappointed was taken as part of the learning process.

Despite failures on many occasions, over 200 innovations were created by the workforce at Rocky Flats in the service of a faster, more efficient and safer clean-up and closure. The development of a highly innovative culture allowed for experiments with hundreds of potential solutions to difficult problems rather than searching for the one right way to approach the tasks.

Meaningful Work

Workforce at Rocky Flats was demotivated, discouraged, and without purpose. Identifying a profound new purpose and meaningfulness for people was a leadership challenge. The project team felt that if the workforce could sense the importance of the scope, dramatic progress could be made.

In the case of Rocky Flats, the meaningful purpose was reinforced in a powerful way, using the incentive system as a key lever.

Other Key Enablers that contributed in the success of Rocky flats:

Goal Clarity

Specificity and clarity of the goal made Rocky Flats mission successful. Clear and unambiguous communication with a diversified work force in absence of clear objectives was important. Seeking clarity was pursued constantly due to which the completion goal always kept on advancing and was finished way ahead of its schedule.

Detailed Planning

The detailed analysis of Rocky Flats facility produced an extremely large variety of activities, all of which were critical in the process of clean-up and closure. The complex project, in other words, was organized into three simple activities—a detailed description of the work scope, estimates of costs, and a timeline. All stakeholders, community groups, regulators, environmentalists, and state officials were engaged in the detailed planning.

"Projectizing" & "Measurement"

Identifying and prioritizing activities was an important first step, but a process had to be put into place for systematic operations. The organization was known for breaking down an entire assignment into a series of projects that had a clearly defined scope, schedule and cost. It is important to realize that in assignments like Rocky Flats, focus on end result could be more beneficial than the process. When work is "projectized" is becomes an objective with a definite time and measurable milestones.

Projectizing also emphasized objective measurement. The Kaiser-Hill's approach to projectizing was more on end results. Outcomes were the focus of the objective measurement system. The management started defining relationships and performance objectively. Instead of managing the contractor, they managed the contract. Instead of establishing personal relationships, they managed business relationships. Instead of relying on subjective evaluation, focus shifted to objective evaluation.

Projectizing was the most useful concept introduced by Kaiser-Hill because it emphasized measurement. It means even if you don't define the right measure, whatever you measure will cause a change in performance. With specific measures, everything linked to these projects revolve around them like the commitment, deadlines, quantum of work, and incentives.

It was made clear to everyone that defining scope, measuring objective performance, and maintaining accountability for outcomes should be everybody's responsibilities and not limiting to senior executives. If the project is expected to be fast paced then it is important to streamline the red tape process. And the best way to achieve it was by open dialog and transparency.

Milestones and Accountability

Multiple tasks and responsibilities can quickly overwhelm a system. To identify and prioritize 500 or more activities is one task but achieving that task was quite a different matter. A key success factor, therefore, was the reduction of those activities into a few key targets or goals. In other words, both detailed micro process and macro targets were necessary for performance to occur. Individual activities had to be identified, prioritized, and budgeted. Clustering them into a few clear objectives and milestones was a means to ensure progress.

Organizational Culture

Culture is the single biggest obstacle to successful organizational change. Organizational culture refers to the values, assumptions, underlying beliefs, and ways of doing things. Rocky Flats valued pride in craftsmanship that had the highest consistency and productivity. It maintained exceptional secrecy even amongst the members of the same family. Such was the practice understandably given the sensitivity of the set up. But when the mission changed the old culture also had to undergo change, or the mission was at risk to fail.

Culture is often considered to be the least important, which according to an ancient proverb means, "Fish discover water last." Attempting for cultural change is difficult because people's identities are under threat. Culture change required attacking almost every part of the existing system—from work processes to relationships to ways of thinking about careers. In doing so a variety of other enablers particularly, collaboration, trust-building, and nurturing human relationships played a very significant role.

Collaboration

Success without synergy and collaboration for the work of this magnitude is unthinkable. Kaiser-Hill was quick to understand the importance and established a task force to do the feasibility study. This task force recommended very aggressive timelines which were subsequently rejected calling them unrealistic, but they created hope that change was possible.

Three major collaborations happened during the project, between the government, community officials and union. To everybody's surprise it worked out just as desired. Presumed inhibitions, conflict of interest and so many other assumptions were clarified when all these agencies sat down and discussed. Everyone realized that their interests weren't different.

Not only were these collaborative relationships useful to overcome resistance to progress, but they also led to better performance than would have occurred in their absence. Collaboration, of course, was not a product of friends or trusted advisers getting together, but the product of adversaries and antagonists being able and willing to work together. They were able to come together and share a common vision.

Trust and Credibility

Collaborative work arrangements and relationships were dependent on a sense of trust among those required to work together. If groups believed that they were being deceived or manipulated, no amount of persuasion, publicity, or promotion would lead to effective cooperation.

Rocky Flats was always under the influence of secrecy culture. Distrust, scepticism and cynicism was very evident. It was important for the team to demonstrate trust, and it was possible by way of achieving the promised results and establishing their credibility.

Rocky Flats team achieved their first milestone ahead of schedule. That was the most significant achievement that demonstrated the team's commitment and rigor towards assignment. There is no way you can do it unless you are really committed to do it. The key to trust-building heavily rests on honesty and openness that will go long with your stakeholders. Culture of transparency and open communication to answer the anxious people of all the groups was sign of transformation. It worked pretty effectively in terms of regaining trust. Maintaining openness, honesty, and transparency was challenging because it was never tried before.

Rigorous Performance

Maintaining pressure to perform was a key part of the positive strategy adopted at Rocky Flats. Demanding timely results, expecting superlative performance, and requiring measurable outcomes were prerequisites for achieving extraordinary success. Establishing rigorous goals, not becoming dissuaded from the targets, and pressing ahead in spite of contrarians were key enablers.

It is one thing to caution against overconfidence, and quite another thing to keep up the pressure and the drive. In other words, pressure for continuing performance remained intense at Rocky Flats until the last day of operation. Successful performance was expected, and penalties were given to those who did not perform and incentivize individual employees when they performed in extraordinary ways.

Conclusion

The big question remains to be answered. What makes the "Impossible Rocky Flats" possible?

At Rocky Flats, however, conflicting strategies like taking care of people along with demanding extraordinary performance, risk-taking and innovation along with careful planning and tight controls; a focus on external stakeholder involvement along with building internal trust and collaboration; and a focus on measurement, milestones, and predictability along with symbolic messages attached to a long-term vision. It is an important insight and learning that simultaneous opposites, tensions, and paradoxes are necessary for extraordinary performance. Leadership played a key role, encouraged revolutionary thinking and innovativeness along with new procedures, and challenging rules for achieving efficiency and effectiveness.

No organization has successfully accomplished this feat. The set of targets achieved were exceptional, be it taking down plutonium building or the process of decontamination. No organization had ever completed this kind of work and that too ahead of schedule and within budgeted cost.

08

Get There Early

About the Author
(Bob Johansen)

Bob Johansen is one of the first social scientists diving into subjects of humans and organizational impacts of the Internet when it was called the ARPANET. Having worked more than thirty years as a forecaster, he also has a deep interest in the future of religion and values.

He served as the president and now is a distinguished fellow at the Institute for the Future.

Bob holds a BS degree from the University of Illinois, which he attended on a basketball scholarship, and a PhD from Northwestern University. He has attended Colgate Rochester Crozer Divinity School, where he studied comparative religions.

He is the author/co-author of twelve books.

Get There Early, Published by Berrett-Koehler Publishers; 2007

Get There Early

Get there early has a very specific meaning. It isn't about speed. Get is an action word, and there implies direction and intent. "Get there" suggests strategy, a direction and a place where you are going, with a purpose and early means at the right time. Usually, getting there early means to gain some advantage, which means avoid rushing, utilizing the opportunity. For organizations, it is about being ahead of your competitors.

Toyota got to the hybrid car market with the Prius at a very good time. Although iPod was not the first digital music player, Apple was the first to make players with great design, ease of use, and functionality. The iPod demonstrates that it is important to get there early but not necessarily to get there first. Success is more about timing than it is about time. Sony got there early with the Walkman for cassette tapes and CDs, but it got there late for digital music players. Get there early means seeing a possible future before others see it.

Organizations that have a get-there-early culture begin meetings on time, even if everyone is not there. Getting there late is just not acceptable. Once a get-there-early or on-time culture is established, most people show up on time—unless truly extenuating circumstances arise. Getting there early respects the time of others.

Getting there early is not about rushing to do as many things as possible. It means you have time to reflect. It's valuable if you have no idea what's going to happen after you arrive. It allows you to get settled, establish a position, and prepare. Getting there early is especially important in times of volatility, uncertainty, complexity, and ambiguity—where figuring out what's going on is not at all easy.

Thinking Ahead

Ten-year forecasting provides a unique perspective that helps you create your own vision for your own organization. Forecasting helps leaders break out and develop new ways. A forecast should be future relevant, not too far and not too near. Forecast is not prediction. A forecast doesn't need to "come true" to be worthwhile, instead it should provoke new thought: new insights, new actions, or new ways of thinking.

Preparing Your Mind

A good leader has a prepared mind for uncertain future. It means being able to hold multiple realities in your mind simultaneously without jumping to judgment too early. Preparing your mind is a readiness exercise. Once you are ready, it is easier to sense where to start. Best sensing happens with an open mind that does not judge, and the only question then that needs to be asked when you arrive early is, "What's going on here?" Sensing prepares your mind for the future and clearly defines when to act and when to wait.

How do you prepare your mind against the external forces that will shape the next ten years? In fact, nobody really knows what the future will look like. It is all assumption based, but what we are sure of is that it will be a world of extreme dilemmas. Forecasting, therefore, is going to be a difficult thing. Leaders will need to take a pause and reflect before responding to the challenges of the future.

Forecasting will help you ride the uncertainty of future. With good sensing capability, leaders can avoid getting hit by something unpleasant. Instead they can ride the waves of change if they are prepared for it.

Forecast Map

For very large organizations, personal empowerment creates a dilemma. How can they engage constructively with the people and their networks who buy their products and services? Consumers are indispensable and cannot be ignored. Their growing indulgence with media is like adding fuel to the fire.

We have observed the three very noticeable behavior patterns of engaged consumers:

- They act with independence but with close-knitted links.
- They adapt to products or services that can be customized to their needs.
- They organize responses and initiatives in ways that are difficult for others to anticipate.

Same is true with engaged employees too. Engaged employees are on a constant look out for avenues that allow them to express themselves. They don't differentiate between work and home because each influences the other. Further forecast suggest that mixing work-life is going to be the reality going forward. It means an engaged employee will be able to contribute better if they bring hobby to work and carry work when performing their hobby. Employers need to be ready for this transition. They need to create people friendly office space, because workforce diversity will dictate the workplace of tomorrow.

Economy, on the other hand, is not going to be the same as olden times. Upscale will not happen as it used to happen traditionally, and it is no more the deciding factor to be successful. Grass-root economy is the new reality, where buyer can be a seller and vice-versa. Each one has the capacity to become large, but it is the personalized approach that is going to decide the winner. Media is going to be the biggest contributor to the success of grass-root economy. As these economies rely heavily on networking, innovative businesses will build on that connectivity to create new wealth.

Networking is key for engaging and scaling. Individuals and organizations can now network through various technologies over distributed locations. These new technologies provide opportunity to individuals to project their identity and presence online. To make best use of this technology leaders will need the networking IQ. It is equally important for them to be familiar and up their skills with blogs, wikis, and other networked media, or it will be hard for them to lead.

The VUCA World

The dangers are characterized by volatility, uncertainty, complexity, and ambiguity. But these same dangers create leadership opportunities that can be described in terms of vision, understanding, clarity, and agility.

It's all about change including both dangerous ruptures and positive innovation. Leaders need to comprehend the dangers and figure out a way to get there early and win. While nobody can predict the future, you can prepare. A prepared mind enhances the chances of success and makes pain manageable.

The VUCA Stories

Army War College – VUCA University

The Army War College is a place where military stars learn to be generals with focus on leadership and strategy. It is a "VUCA University" for life-and-death dilemmas. The story that introduces learning on the go with several other challenges, which no conventional training can offer.

One afternoon in July 2003, a young army commander led his battalion into the center of a town in northern Iraq. The orders were to make peace with local religious leaders. Unrest looming in the country and hatred towards the Americans were clear indication for possible violence.

While soldiers marched along a main road, Iraqi men started gathering in the street with a threat of becoming a mob. With growing hostility and anger, the crowd appeared to be very intimidating.

The commander sensed that the mood in the crowd was very threatening. On raising his arm, the platoon stopped. He was left with very little choice with regard to his mission – either retreat or take position, but none were appropriate. Violence would destabilize the mission and retreat would hurt the dignity. He was caught in a dilemma with all bad options at his disposal.

Instead of reacting, he took a moment to focus. He improvised an alternate approach, part strategy and part tactic, neither surrender nor aggression. He ordered his men to smile, raise their weapons in the air and turn their barrels down, and to kneel on the ground. They had not laid down their weapons or lowered their heads. They could still respond militarily on short notice if necessary. But their gesture was enough to neutralize the aggression in the crowd. The commander's response defused a potentially dangerous situation, avoided violence, and allowed for the successful completion of his mission on a return visit.

This story introduces a strategic learning situation. How can organizations teach leaders to deal with dilemmas that cannot be anticipated? The leader in this story was ready in this life-threatening moment, and he reacted instinctively. How can leaders learn to sense what's going on and come up with a successful response? In the VUCA world, leaders should look to engage in new ways of thinking and acting, and converting challenges into opportunity.

Mohammad Yunus: Evolution of Grameen Bank

In another example of VUCA, the story of Muhammad Yunus, Nobel Prize winner, who lived with the poor and saw an opportunity in the crises. Bangladesh was going through a turmoil, where no economic measure was found to be helping the cause. It was then, Yunus ideated the concept of financial institution, and created micro-finance module in the form of Grameen Bank. Yunus saw the strength of social capital and pitched it against the financial collateral. He made this model part of the people's daily life, where each one becomes invested and interested in others' success. Using the new principles of micro-finance, Yunus reversed the age-old vicious cycle of low income, low saving, and low investment into a virtuous cycle of more income, more savings and more investment. The VUCA world of poverty in Bangladesh is now being turned around with a combination of vision, understanding, clarity, and agility.

The New VUCA
(Vision, Understanding, Clarity, Agility)

Vision means having a clear intent. It is much more important than foresight, since vision seeks to create a future; it also creates space for innovation. Muhammad Yunus said in 1996, "One day our grandchildren will go to the museums to see what poverty was." That's vision, bold and clear, and most importantly, he did not begin with this vision, it simply emerged.

Understanding begins with listening, which is the basis for trust. The VUCA world creates an urgency to act quickly, but sometimes it is a false sense of urgency. The best leaders have the presence and calm to listen before talking, to open an opportunity for deep understanding. Understanding is a prerequisite to trust, and trust is vital to building community.

The VUCA world rewards clarity because people are so confused that they grasp at anything that helps them make sense out of the chaos. It is the leader's role to clarify the complexity, and good leaders do it very effectively. Clarity is good, and we should strive for it. The thoughtful leader's quest is to be both, clear and accurate, simple but not simplistic.

In an ambiguous world, surprises should be no surprise. Surrendering to ambiguity will lead to paralysis and confusion; rather Leaders should stay agile and be responsive to attack. Networking surpasses the rigid hierarchies; it knows no boundary and helps you stay agile.

We all have our personal VUCA moments, when our own life becomes volatile, uncertain, complex, and ambiguous. Personal crises hit everyone at some point. In these moments, we are challenged to respond. The VUCA world is all around us, with more or less intensity. Those of us in the less intense environments can learn from those in the more extreme ones. The choice to choose, whether to fall prey to the old VUCA or move ahead and get future ready with new VUCA always lies with us.

What's Different About Dilemmas?

Many senior executives are simply not prepared for the dilemma-laden environment of today, let alone tomorrow. So how do you prepare your mind to win when you are faced with dilemmas?

The world of dilemmas requires us to shift our words and our thinking to embrace both. When we're dealing with dilemmas, we need words that can be used with flexibility and the ability to avoid taking our words too seriously. Getting past your dilemmas requires an ability to hold complexity in your mind and staying indifferent. With dilemmas, you need to pay attention to what's behind the words, what's beneath the data. When stuck in a dilemma, individual's ability to control and not pushing for a solution, considering it as a problem, is the greatest quality a leader can have.

Problems and dilemmas require different kinds of engagement processes. A problem is "a question or a puzzle that needs to be solved." Problems are there to be solved and you get a sense of accomplishment. But dilemmas have many options for response, neither simple nor straight. It is beyond yes/no, and attempting a one dimensional solution is invitation to bigger unknown problems. Dilemmas are messy and frustrating, but they are also fertile ground for new insights and new inspiration, to create strategy that succeeds.

Leaders need to learn to live with and even embrace dilemmas. Dilemmas can be a source of insight and inspiration if you can figure out how to engage with and learn from them. Leaders need an ability to hold, listen, and learn—while resisting the temptation to know too soon.

Problems can be solved with data and analytics, but dilemmas need stories. Data and analytics address the what; stories probe the why. Data reflects rationality; stories reflect emotion. Data reveals answers; stories reveal questions. Questions, it turns out, are more useful than answers when it comes to dilemmas.

The Story of Silicon Valley

The story of Silicon Valley exhibits a great dilemma between the "culture of ideas" and the "culture of money". The 'culture-of-ideas' people, love ideas and love to exchange them, trusting that they will get back even better ideas in return. They are convinced that their ideas can have an impact. Meanwhile, the 'culture-of-money' people, are focused on minting money through the commercialization of technology and ideas. They are driven by greed and an irrational quest for wealth.

Regardless of their motives they both are dependent on each other. Innovation and technology needs money to bring their ideas to life, while money needs ideas and innovation to attract investors. None likes the other, but both recognize the need to accommodate. The tension between ideas and money is what energizes and fuels innovation at Silicon Valley; therefore this dilemma will continue till Valley exists.

The Best Way to Learn in the VUCA World

The VUCA world is constantly shifting. It takes a very flexible approach to learn how to lead in this world. Ambiguity can be satisfying and productive if you are prepared for it. Immersion is a deeper way to learn than reading, listening, or even seeing. It can help leaders see things from a different perspective. It can help you become agile and extract strategic insights.

The uncertainties of the future, especially in volatile times, can be energizing in a positive way, or they can instill fear. Both are forms of anticipation and anticipation is driven by vision. A belief that the world can be better in some way if we perform the right actions. Such vision leans eagerly toward the future. Both the threats and the opportunities are real. Playing not to lose, however, is rarely a good strategy in any game—or in any aspect of life.

The best leaders will be able to thrive in a world of ambiguity, if they can embrace uncertainty. In a VUCA world, there is no script for leaders to memorize. Success will require flexibility and agility—like that of a great athlete or performer—within a firm structure of values and discipline. We all have to perform, and we need practice time. The prepared will perform more effectively and efficiently over time.

Sensing Is a Virtue

Leaders sense the future, drawing out insights and acting with informed sensibility. Leaders develop their own ways to sense dilemmas, engage with them, and develop flexible responses. Leaders also teach others about sensing. Think of sensing as listening, listening to the world around you, and listening for your inner voice of innovation. Sensing is listening for the future, hearing something that others don't yet hear.

VUCA! Beware of Problem Solvers

Action is the home court of the problem solver. Problem solvers love to act, and they especially love to act quickly and decisively. Leaders need to think twice about problem-solving actions in order to engage constructively. The key here is to recognize the difference between a problem and a dilemma as early as possible. If in doubt, assume you are dealing with a dilemma. If as the situation unfolds, it turns out that you are dealing with a solvable problem, all you need to do is solve it and move on. On the other hand, if you mistake a dilemma for a problem, there may be no way out.

Accept the VUCA World

Action is not just about doing, but being in the state of readiness, and foresight helps create readiness. We all need to accept uncertainty, not avoid it or pretend to avoid. Strategy and plans are great, but surprises should be assumed. If you get there early, you are more likely to be prepared for a threat, an opportunity, or a mix of both.

The future world, however, will be dominated by dilemmas. There will be no place to run. Although it is impossible to predict, it is relatively easy to provoke. The more constructive the provocation, the more likely that you can create a strategy that allows you to get there early. Future sensing, strategy, humility, and a sense of humor should all go together. "I don't know" is the only honest response in some situations, and it is perfectly acceptable. "I don't know" can be the starting point for a constructive conversation. Humility is engaging; arrogance is not.

Getting there early is not about more rushing around; it's about more wisdom. We need time to consider our options, time to understand. We must, as hard as it is, reconsider how we experience time. It's not just about time; it's about timing. Leadership will be defined by how we "take time" or "make time" to reflect and understand what's going on around us.

Getting there early, the Foresight to Insight to Action Cycle, and the creative combination of vision, understanding, clarity, and agility can help leaders resolve the continuing challenge that opened this book, the tension between judging too soon and deciding too late.

09

The Empress Has No Clothes

About the Authors
(Joyce Roché & Alexander Kopelman)

Author, Mentor and Businesswoman, Joyce Roché is an ideal for working women. Being in the corporates for more than 25 years she mentors them in finding their voices and taking bold career risks to progress. She is the CEO of Girls Inc., a non-profit organization, whose mission is to inspire all girls to be strong, smart, and bold.

She broke the glass ceiling by becoming Avon's first African American female vice president, the first African American vice president of marketing, and the company's first vice president of global marketing.

Joyce is the author of three books. She is the recipient of the Legacy Award during Black Enterprise magazine's Women of Power Summit and Distinguished Alumna Award from Columbia University Women in Business.

A graduate of Dillard University in New Orleans and an MBA from Columbia University, she has also successfully completed Stanford University's Senior Executive Program. Joyce holds honorary doctorate degrees from Dillard University and North Adams State College.

Alexander Kopelman is the Co-founder, President & CEO of the Children's Arts Guild. A writer and advocate, he has devoted twenty-five years to advancing social justice and personal empowerment.

With a very special passion for supporting young people, he helps them overcome the limiting effects of outmoded societal stereotypes on individual development. Alex brings a wealth of experience in gender-specific youth development, having served as the Director of Marketing of Girls Inc., the premier girls' empowerment organization in the US and Canada, for over twelve years.

Alex has authored and co-authored ten books.

The Empress Has No Clothes, Published by Berrett-Koehler Publishers; 2013

The Empress Has No Clothes

A lot of us build our careers believing that titles or money will help us get respect and to some extent they even do. Wouldn't it be great if these people can work on who they are as human beings rather than what they do?

Ask yourself: "What am I trying to prove? To whom? And why?"

I began to feel anxious about my ability to make my way in the world and to succeed. Would I really be able to compete with all these smart kids whose families had so many more resources than mine did? Would I be able to continue my education and work at the same time? These were the questions that increasingly occupied my mind.

I remember the days in high school, when I felt I had to hide my reality, laid the foundation for the fear of being discovered. The disconnect between the inside and the outside quickly became a burden.

Although I went on to have a very successful career, I was never really able to rid myself of the doubts: Am I prepared for this?

Am I ready? Am I able to do this? Yet I kept going into the tougher and tougher areas. I think there was always this pull to prove myself. If I didn't do the hardest thing, I felt like I would be left out. But even as I succeeded, there was no respite. No matter how well I did, the thought of proving myself all over again would never leave me. To quiet this thought of self-doubt you need to start by looking at your strengths and challenges. What are the special skills you have? What are the qualities that attract others to you? What makes you the person you are?

Dr. Pauline Clance, the pioneer in impostor syndrome research, explains the difference between impostor feelings and insecurity. People who suffer from the impostor syndrome tend to be very successful, whereas people with high insecurity tend to be less accomplished. Impostor feelings include questions about one's ability to compete, while insecurity is primarily about one's abilities.

People who experience impostor feelings like to take on greater challenges, to always reach for the next level, which then triggers the concerns about their ability to measure up. It's as if once we get on that treadmill, we find it very difficult to stop. One of the paradoxes of the impostor syndrome is that the people who suffer from it tend to be ambitious and accomplished.

Know Your Fear

Success puts us in unfamiliar situations, and it is natural to feel anxious. Social status is a major source of impostor fears, but it is just "bloated nothingness." It is essential that you clarify your own values and look to build connections with people who share those values, regardless of their social class.

Living an authentic life will help you minimize worries about not fitting in, no matter how high you move up the social ladder.

The terrible irony of the impostor syndrome is that it shows up most intensely to make us question whether we are worthy of our accomplishments at the very moment we succeed. And since it is a form of social anxiety, it forces us to compare ourselves to our new peer group—to people who have succeeded in a similar sphere—and to worry about the ways in which we do and don't fit in. Most often, we focus on the non-negotiable aspects of ourselves, those things we cannot change.

Analyze Your Success

Develop a written inventory of your skills, accomplishments, and experiences to build an understanding of your success and begin to exercise your skills. It is reasonable to be fearful—to feel uncertain to some extent—when you are doing something for the first time. Who you are and how you are, affects how you see yourself as a leader and how people experience you as a leader. The fact is that women and people of color— and younger women and people of color in particular—face significant hurdles in being accepted as leaders.

Success at a young age can be very disorienting, but it is a wonderful feeling to have the validation of being entrusted with responsibility and authority. On the other hand, impostor fears rise up and make us wonder whether we are actually experienced enough to handle the responsibility. People who experience the impostor syndrome are, on the whole, very driven and ambitious. You succeed not just because you work hard but also because you have the ability to do the job. That's difficult to remember, though, when that hard work gets you to the next level of achievement and the fears rise up.

Our fear tells us that if we put in the extra hours, prepare better, and sacrifice more, we will have earned our place at the table. The same fear, however, constantly reminds us that we are from the wrong side of the tracks, that we don't look like everyone else, that we are not as smart, and so on.

Question Your Work Habits

If you are like most people who experience impostor fears, you are likely to compensate for feeling unworthy by working harder than anyone else around you.

1. Debra Lee: Discovering My Path

Debra Lee went to an all-Black junior and high school. It was a great experience because of dedicated teachers, who instilled in them the faith that they could be anything they wanted to be.

In her college days, she ended up going to Brown. Going in, there wasn't any fear of competing. She owed all her confidence to the training from the teachers of high school. Intellectually, she felt challenged and excited. She had a really great positive college experience.

As she approached her graduation, she thought of going to law school in California, so that she could be near her boyfriend. When she went to talk to the dean, he proposed an unpleasant option to her, either to apply at Harvard or Yale. In spite of her initial rejection and objection, she ended up at Harvard.

That's when the impostor syndrome showed up big time. She had a white friend whom she had met in the second year. When she learned that Debra had gotten into Harvard, she said jokingly that Debra had gotten in because she was an affirmative action case. Harvard is Harvard, and supposedly only the best and brightest go there. Debra had gone to Brown without any self-doubt, but with Harvard, she was suddenly anxious. She was worried to discover whether she made a mistake. She kept on thinking that she wasn't going to be successful and would let her family down, and her community down, and her race down.

Because of this fear she never joined study groups and did not socialize with her classmates, instead she started spending more time with friends from the medical school, so that she could get away from the law school.

That first year, she ended up hating law school, feeling very alienated and not learning law either. She couldn't waste this opportunity and drop out. So, she applied to the Kennedy School of Government and got in for the joint program. She did one year of law school, one year at the Kennedy School, and then two years at both, finishing with a master's in public policy. Even with all the heartache of the first year, she did really well in her studies and no longer felt like an impostor.

Race is a powerful trigger for impostor feelings. Whether consciously or not, people often make assumptions about others based on the color of their skin. The important thing for each of us to come to terms with is how to be in relation to the assumptions people may make about us.

Debra's story of losing her emotional balance in law school and then regaining it when she found a more authentic path is a vivid illustration of how impostor fears based on race can materialize when we lose connection with ourselves. At those times, it is no longer other people's assumptions we have to grapple with but our own. Remember, it is your essence that defines who you are.

Dominant Culture

The terrible irony of the impostor syndrome is that it shows up most intensely to make us question whether we are worthy of our accomplishments at the very moment we succeed. It forces us to compare ourselves to people who have succeeded in a similar sphere—and to worry about the ways in which we do and don't fit in.

2. Katherine Windsor: What Does It Take to Feel Successful?

In my doctoral research, I wanted to understand better how young women think about success. For young women, in particular, there is a real gap between what we encourage them to believe and how things are in the world. We tell them that they can do anything. So people go into their careers and chase their ambitions with the expectation that this is true. But, in fact, the sociopolitical domain is very different. There are very few women who enjoy the privilege of having power and authority and who receive top salaries. This feeds a sense of uncertainty about whether you have what it takes to be successful.

Katherine is a white Christian woman, with a successful career and a fulfilling family life. And yet, she struggled with impostor feelings in a profound way.

In her first job, she was hired to coach lacrosse at a boarding school. At the first departmental faculty meeting, when she was introduced, one of her colleague said loudly, "My goodness, I have sweaters older than you." So that was how she was introduced to teaching. It only got harder when she was named a department chair a relatively short time after.

She dreaded telling people what she did as part of her accomplishments, because she constantly had to answer the question, "How did you get that job?" In fact, that question followed all her life career. She went on to become the head of school at an independent school in Boston at the age of thirty. This was so unheard of that a group of parents challenged her appointment, alleging that her candidature had not been properly vetted. Ten years later, when she left the school, they named the arts and athletic wing after her name.

In her mid-forties after being the head of school for nearly fifteen years, whenever she introduces herself she still gets the same response. Some people don't register her title and sometime during the conversation ask, "And what do you do at Miss Porter's?" Others look surprised and say things like, "How old are you?" or "Do you have children?" or "How did you get the job?"

We say over and over, "You can do anything and be anybody you want to be." But they look at the experiences that their mothers have had and those of women in positions of leadership and power, and they don't buy it. They don't buy this idea that if you work hard, and you go to the right college, and you get the right internship, and you pay your dues, you are going to have a successful and fulfilling life.

Even when I talk to them about finding a life for themselves that's fulfilling and purposeful, they feel that it's harder than ever. Success is still being defined by the dominant culture, and that sets up powerful internal conflicts for the individual.

Learning to Know Yourself

Developing a realistic sense of your own strengths and limitations is a critical step in confronting your fears. The next time someone compliments you on something you have done well, see if you can put aside your habitual response and allow the information to sink in.

As we succeed and advance in our careers, we inevitably encounter situations that challenge our abilities. We also cross paths with honest critics, powerful competitors, and out-and-out enemies. Running into roadblocks can cause feelings of doubt and unworthiness, but it also provides opportunities for true growth. The real difficulty with the impostor syndrome is that it makes us hungry for external validation. Silencing our fears becomes possible when we begin to accept our actual strengths and weaknesses and to learn how to derive internal validation from that self-knowledge.

I got to know Val Ackerman, the founding president of the Women NBA (WNBA) and former president of USA Basketball, when she joined the Girls Inc. board of directors.

When I began to write and speak about my experience with the impostor syndrome, Val told me that she has also struggled with these feelings, particularly with respect to her intellectual abilities. She also spoke very movingly about her own journey of conquering the feelings through the process of self-discovery.

3. Val Ackerman: If I Can't Be the Smartest, I'll Be the Hardest-Working

I grew up in New Jersey, in a suburb of Trenton, the elder of two kids. My parents were solidly middle-class. My mom worked in state government in New Jersey, and my dad was a high school athletic director, and later a gym teacher and a referee at the high school level. He was all sports, and he was really my inspiration. He was very encouraging and took my athletic interest as seriously as he took my brother's. Both my parents were great about always supporting us in pursuing what we wanted to do.

I became interested in sports at a very young age. In the late 1960s there weren't many opportunities for girls. I was in high school when I got my first chance to play on a team. I was so excited, I played field hockey, basketball, and ran track. Even though I loved sports, my lifelong dream, from an early age, was to become a lawyer. I am not really sure why. It just sounded interesting and lofty. So, after a year in Europe, I came back to the United States and went to law school at UCLA.

I was very eager to get a job in sports coming out of law school. After two years, I was fortunate to land a job in the legal department at the National Basketball Association. It was a dream come true for me to have that professional opportunity. Everything just came together, my passion for basketball and my professional aspirations.

But I had a really hard time with my feelings of intellectual intimidation. At every stage of my life, I was surrounded by really smart people. In college, there were a lot of bright students. In law school, you are dealing with really brainy classmates. At my law firm, there were many brilliant people. And at the NBA, we had some of the sharpest people in sports, led by David Stern, who is supremely intelligent.

My way of coping with these feelings was to work harder than anyone else. I said to myself that since I wasn't the smartest person in the room, I would be the most diligent one. On every assignment I put in extra time, did as much research as possible, and made sure I understood all the details. Before every meeting, I prepared for hours. The preparation paid off, and I did well in the intellectually challenging climate of the NBA. I started out as a staff lawyer and then moved over to the commissioner's office. I worked on a variety of projects, but my role was not very clearly defined. This wasn't really an issue until I had my two children. At that point, I went through a very difficult time professionally.

They didn't expect me to come back after my pregnancies. I felt I had to prove to them that even though I was a mother of infants, I was really serious about my career. There was some real tension that I had to fight through. I was already used to being one of the hardest-working people in the room, so I wasn't afraid of the challenge. With time, my colleagues came to see just how committed I was to my career and to basketball.

My major break came when the commissioner wanted to look at women's basketball in a serious way. He asked me to lead that effort, which resulted in our supporting the women's Olympic basketball team at the Atlanta games. That was the testing ground to get a sense of the level of interest in a women's league. We got a lot of encouragement from fans and sponsors, and eventually launched the WNBA in the summer of 1997. I was truly honored to be selected and to serve as president of the league for the first eight years.

When I became the president of the WNBA, I didn't have the same kinds of doubts I had experienced earlier in my career. It felt like a cause, and I saw the real sense of purpose and a clearly defined leadership role for myself. And, of course, it was exciting and intimidating, all at once, because it was new. I also began to acknowledge my personal strengths, beyond just being a hard worker. I recognized that I have a humility that helps me make good decisions, because I don't think I am always right and therefore take other people's opinions into account. And most importantly, I gave myself credit for being good with people, for knowing how to build a team and make people feel empowered.

I think it was when I began to appreciate these qualities in myself that I understood just how much I had grown. Building the self-awareness to figure out how you can maximize what you can contribute based on your strengths is a critical part of professional development. I always say to young people:

There are always going to be people out there who are smarter than you, and people who are going to work harder than you. You may not be able to make yourself smarter. And, beyond a certain point, you may not be able to work any harder. But if you look at yourself, you can figure out what your special strengths are. You may be a great public speaker. You may have personal charm. Or you might have a wonderful sense of humor. Whatever your strengths are, find them, and put them to good use.

Whatever coping mechanisms we develop to help us deal with our impostor fears, sooner or later, we reach their limitations. For me that moment of truth came when I realized, after stepping into my new vice president role at Avon, that I simply could not work any harder. At that point, I had to evaluate honestly my ability to do the job. That was the beginning for me of learning how to manage the impostor syndrome from a position of strength. We do not recognize our essential worth and are therefore constantly terrified that we will be found lacking. The pursuit of validation becomes a driving need, often eclipsing other parts of our lives and ourselves. The process of conquering these fears begins with stopping to look at your life and asking what might be missing for you. Ask whether you are satisfied. Are there dimensions you want to add? Do you need more balance? Ultimately, the question has to be, "What do I value about myself?"

Listen to your Heart

Your essence is what makes you who you are. Connecting with that spiritual essence is a critical element in moving toward conquering the impostor syndrome.

After leaving Carson, I needed some time to decide what I wanted to do next. In my fifties, I realized that, this was the last phase of my full-time working career. And I wanted to make sure that it would be meaningful and enjoyable. I had the luxury of time and the emotional tools I had acquired in my struggle with the impostor syndrome.

In my search for internal validation, I began by reminding myself of the journey that had gotten me where I was. I was painfully honest with myself about what I was and wasn't good at. I pushed myself to distinguish between the things I liked and those I really didn't like but I pretended to. And most importantly, I thought about what I truly valued in my life.

Through this reflection, it became apparent that proving myself was no longer the sole objective. When I left Avon, what I wanted was another challenge, and everything else— location, industry—was wide open. Now, I wanted not only a professional challenge but also a position that was congruent with who I was as a person. With that, two priorities emerged: I wanted to be with a company that had really strong values. I also wanted to stay geographically close enough to the people in my life to maintain intimate connections.

My commitment to these priorities was put to the test when I had the opportunity at Starbucks. But the job was in Seattle, and that was just too far from everybody who was important to me. I stuck to my guns and did not pursue the opportunity further.

As I was sorting through my professional options, I used some of my spare time to do a bit of pro bono work for a couple of local non-profit organizations. Ernesta Procope, the storied African American businesswoman, who was a board member of the company, had recommended me to serve on a corporate advisory board at Queens College. I didn't have any connection to Queens College and was very concerned about the time commitment, but I was honored to have been singled out by Ernesta and signed on.

From the start, I found the conversation fascinating. We were discussing the real-life applications of education. Our role was to help the college understand how best to prepare students for successful careers in the business world by sharing our observations of the kinds of skills newly graduated employees tended to lack. I quickly realized that I was making a real contribution and having an impact. I was getting great satisfaction from the work I was doing with these non-profits.

As I thought about all this, I remembered Aunt Rose say, during my growing up, "Joyce, to get where you're going, you've got to be strong enough to listen to your heart." Suddenly, I could see myself leaving the corporate world and devoting myself to a social mission that was important to me.

4. Mary Wagner: A Lesson in Staying True to Yourself

A critical element in moving toward conquering the impostor syndrome is connecting with your spiritual—essential—self. I am not talking about religious faith, necessarily, but the sense of belonging to something larger than ourselves we get from tuning into the voices of our hearts and being wholly ourselves in the world.

As Mary describes it, it is the fabric of your life—that which not only mirrors faithfully who you are but also accepts, values, and celebrates you. You are at the center of your life's fabric, and self-acceptance is an essential element in coming to know that you are not an impostor.

When we overcome our fears, we begin to experience the "joy, zest, and power" of our accomplishments. None of us know our full potential, and it is a real disservice to ourselves and to society if we allow self-doubt to keep us from finding out. When we help each other confront the challenges of our lives, we all grow. Share your joy, zest, and power, and you will be repaid thousand-fold.

10

Fear Your Strengths

About the Author
(Robert E. Kaplan/Robert B. Kaiser)

President of Kaplan DeVries Inc., Robert E. Kaplan specializes in assessing leaders for selection and for development. Coming up with a 360 survey (SKILL scope for Managers), he also developed the idea for a different breed of 360, the patented Leadership Versatility Index, which he and Robert B. Kaiser developed and commercialized.

An honorary senior fellow at the Center for Creative Leadership, he has a B.A. and Ph.D. from Yale University.

Robert B. Kaiser's subject of interest is leadership. Robert is the author, co-author, and editor of five books, and a highly respected public speaker. He and Robert E. Kaplan were awarded a patent for the revolutionary features in their next-generation assessment instrument, the Leadership Versatility Index.

His work is a blend of behavioral science and extensive consulting work that ranges from coaching high potentials to helping CEOs. In 2012, he formed Kaiser Leadership Solutions to create tools for assessment and development that set a new standard for innovation and impact.

Robert received an M.S. in Organizational Psychology from Illinois State University; the College of Arts and Sciences named him alumnus of the year in 2007.

Fear Your Strengths, Published by Berrett-Koehler Publishers in 2013

Fear Your Strengths

Nobody ever thinks that their strength can go against them. Like most organizations, when they do performance appraisals, they either assess whether their deputies were able to meet expectations or exceed expectations. Unfortunately, over-doing is never notified. When leaders consider their strength as the only truth and ignore the other, they start showing lopsidedness in their style. As Aristotle emphasized: "Anybody can become angry or give money, but to be angry with or to give money to the right person, and in the right amount, and at the right time, and for the right purpose, and in the right way—this is not within everybody's power and is not easy."

Leaders often use their strengths, and overuse to the extent possible for obtaining the desired results. These styles could be; being forceful and straightforward or being consensus-seeking or being overly respectful.

1. Enron Scandal

There is no better case of corrupted strengths than that of Jeffrey Skilling, Enron's company president who scripted the great

Enron scandal. Skilling's wild ambition for growth pushed him to unethical and illegal work practices that eventually resulted in the downfall.

Jeffrey Skilling was one of the most brilliant and creative executives inducted into Enron to head its trading operation. Being a visionary, he sensed the opportunity to convert Enron's contracts to buy and sell natural gas into financial instruments. In his lust for building business, he went overboard, over ruling all legitimate procedures. He went to the extent of orchestrating false balance sheet and company's financial condition, only to be discovered later that Enron's balance sheet shows borrowing of only $13 billion as against $38 billion.

Skilling started building his team by picking people who were intelligent and did not pay attention to soft skills. Lacking operational experience, Skilling could not appreciate the realities of this industry. Problems multiplied when Skilling ignored Enron's Risk Assessment and Control (RAC) group and went on to break the rules to meet his motive. While many were responsible, eventually it was Skilling who master-minded.

The overuse of strength spares none. Every leader possesses one strong tendency that carries with it the risk of being too strong. When this lopsidedness takes hold it can become chronic, deeply habitual and in the worst cases virulent.

The Yin-Yang

The yin-yang symbol represents this perfectly, showing two black-and-white teardrop shapes, curled and flowing into each other, continually adapting to each other to form a continuous and complete circle.

It supports the leadership dualities that have both complementary and opposing characteristics, like the sky and earth, day and night, water and fire. Neither takes prominence or precedence, but each is useful and valid and reinforces the other. And likewise leaders are not strangers to the idea that skill sets come in pairs. Despite this awareness, all their lives they have to defend their overuse resulting in lopsidedness in their style: like if I am bold, I can never retreat.

There are two core dualities that confront all leaders: combining the need to be forceful and enabling or combining strategic focus and operational focus. It's like strategic leadership positioning the organization for the future, and operational leadership is about getting results in the short term.

2. Carla Middleton and Billy Peoples

Carla Middleton, first woman president at a liberal arts college, was a very forceful leader. Having a mind of her own, she could never make good use of the intellect and energy of other people. Within a few months of her into that post, she made some successful contributions, but unfortunately she earned mild admiration and no friends.

The exact opposite was Billy Peoples, great believer in enabling other people's talents, a great listener, who excelled at making decisions by consensus. He always treated other people with respect and cared for their self-esteem. But Billy's overused humility prevented him from making tough personnel decisions and in the process lost out on making an impression.

Two different leadership styles and both tarnished their strengths. Their lopsidedness jeopardized their own careers. "Forceful" and "enabling" constitute broad classes of leadership behavior. Each of those behaviors can be either virtues or vices, if taken to the extreme.

The simple fact is that both viewpoints are valid. To lead means making your presence felt, taking a stand, setting high expectations, and making tough calls. However, without delegating responsibility, showing appreciation, and providing support, it is ineffective.

Strategic and Operational Leadership

Research shows that strategically oriented leaders show aggressiveness and vision, but aren't grounded. On the other hand, operationally oriented leaders relied more on their focus and systematic approach, but lacked broad vision and risk-taking ability.

Once again, "strategic" and "operational" are broad categories that can be broken down into specific pairs of behaviors that can be either virtues or vices if overdone. Strategic leaders tend to focus on setting direction, growing and driving innovation, whereas operational leaders tend to focus on execution, efficiency and process. Each of these leadership virtues may turn into vices when taken to unnecessary extremes.

None of the leadership skills work, unless a leader is versatile. A versatile leader is the one who just can't afford to see things in one dimension. You have to see the big picture and the little picture. Zooming in and out should be at the back of your mind. Just as Steve Jobs did, learn to overcome the paradox and become more versatile.

Steve Jobs and John Sculley at Apple provide a classic example. When Mike Markkula, president Apple, decided to step down, he felt that Jobs was young and lacked the discipline and temperament to run the company. Instead, he hired Sculley, then president of PepsiCo, for the job. Sculley was new to the computer industry, but Apple management trusted Sculley's background from conventional consumer business. They felt that it would give the company an image of greater stability. Living to his promise, Sculley transformed Apple into a household name and grew the company significantly, within couple of years of his taking over. However, with rising power struggle between Jobs and Sculley, the board of directors decided to release Jobs of all operational responsibilities. Jobs then left Apple to found NeXT Computer. In the meantime, Sculley was seen struggling with his product vision, and slowly things started crumbling. Despite having grown the company from $600 million a year to more than $8 billion, Apple's stock did not improve. Management decided to part ways with Sculley, and his tenure with Apple ended in 1993.

Soon, Apple purchased NeXT in 1996, and Jobs returned as Apple's interim CEO. But his focus was different this time. He immediately concentrated on returning Apple to profitability by terminating ill-fated projects. Eventually, Jobs led Apple's return to cutting-edge dominance with elegantly designed and cleverly branded home-run products such as the iPod, iPhone, and iPad, and became the full-time CEO. Jobs' second tenure with Apple was clearly no longer the one-dimensional visionary who founded the company. His experiences with NeXT and Pixar made him a more versatile leader.

Some leaders worry that becoming versatile will take away their distinctness. But an empowering leader who learns to be more assertive is also capable of empathy. Even Steve Jobs realized he could have become a better leader by modulating his forcefulness and intensity. Toward the end of his life, reflecting on his infamously harsh style, he admitted, "I was hard on people sometimes, probably too hard." Rather leaders who develop versatility never lose their edge.

Mindset

Everyone has set ways of viewing the world. Very early in our lives we learn to associate ourselves with the truth that we believe to be. It is our experiences that contribute to this belief, and we tend to be always governed by it. These experiences create the lopsidedness in our behavior, and it gets embedded into us stronger and deeper.

A leader always desires to succeed and fears failure. This mindset leads him to micromanage with an assumption that "I should know everything all the time". Such preoccupation makes them insecure, creates pressure and affects their ability to function.

Mindset and behavior are parallel tracks toward improvement. Mindset change is difficult because it needs to deal with your subconscious defense mechanisms. When you work towards improving both your internal and external persona, the chances of retaining that behavior is longer. The only question you need to answer is: How committed are you to improve?

The best way to progress towards this change is by recognizing the signs of overuse of your strengths. Great performers deal with the overuse by slowing down the action so that they can modulate their natural reflex reactions. They continuously work upon their inner and outer self to overcome the deep-rooted effects of strengths and lopsidedness. But the trouble in countering an overused behavior is because leaders see it as an all-or-nothing choice.

Andre Agassi, the eight-time Grand Slam tennis champion, revealed that he never wanted to take up tennis as his career because of the constant pressure to perform. His friend and coach, Brad Gilbert, told him: "You don't have to be the best in the world every time you go out there. Right now, by trying for the perfect shot with every ball, you're stacking the odds against yourself. When you chase perfection, you're chasing something that doesn't exist. You're making everyone around you miserable. You're making yourself miserable." Agassi adjusted his mental and physical game as per Gilbert's guidance and went on to win six of his eight Grand Slams.

Positive feedback is an invaluable tool for modulating an overused strength that negative feedback does not. As Agassi later said: "I find peace in his claim that perfectionism is voluntary. I always assumed perfectionism was an inborn part of me."

Changing yourself is an admirable exercise in self-control. But it is wise to team up with people who can aid your efforts. Let's say, if you identify characteristics of strong personality getting too intense and difficult to approach, have couple of team mates who can send you the warnings signals that you are off track. It basically means that other people can help leaders correct their dysfunctional lopsided tendencies.

Conclusion:

To become a more nearly complete leader, we believe you need to do three things: accept yourself, test yourself, and offset yourself.

Accept Yourself

To grow and improve isn't knowing yourself. It is the ability to connect with the reality of how you lead and knowing what is not effective about your qualities of leadership. Self-acceptance means internalizing what others appreciate about us. To accept praise, it is necessary to accept our fears; it is to be courageously objective about yourself.

Test Yourself

The accumulation of new experience is a sign of growing and improving. It is the positive attitude of doing your best in every situation, big or small, which helps you grow as a leader and a person. There are 100 billion brain cells that continue to regenerate and help adapt to new experiences, making us better at dealing with paradox and complexity.

Doing something repeatedly that you had been avoiding is known as desensitization, a proven technique for getting over a phobia. Problems will appear to be opportunities; similarly adversity is great only if we view it from the right perspective. The habit of venturing out of your comfort zone will prepare you for the unknown test.

Offset Yourself

Being effective in your role doesn't have to all come from you. Indeed, it can't all come from you. One way to offset yourself is to put counterbalancing people and processes in place and then allow them to influence you, even when it hurts, without being too resistant or too receptive to them. The other way to offset yourself is to do what leaders everywhere know to do, compensate for your weaknesses, meaning you must value what you lack.

Acknowledgments

The idea germinated, when our common interest of reading and the prevalent problem of lack time got to us. This set us thinking to find a solution which could be useful to one and all. And 'Take A Break' was born......

The deliberations and discussions amongst us began. Like puzzle pieces falling in place, from different Genres we got to one. The management getting the final vote to start off with.

We would like to thank our Mentors who paved way for this insightful thinking.

Our family who has been the source of constant inspiration and encouragement. Giving us the courage to pursue our dreams and being the most supportive anyone could ever be. We couldn't have come this far if it wasn't for them.

An amazing group of friends who gave their valuable inputs from the pilot study for this book.

Rajeev Pillai and Lipi Sathwara for all their support and help through the way.

This dream of doing our bit for the society was well supported by the Berrett-Koehler Team. We will forever be grateful to Ms. Kate for giving us our first break.

Our readers for choosing this book and look forward to their support in all our future endeavours.

Last but not the least, we thank God almighty for orchestrating this journey and making things possible.

Chapter Insights

Book 1: Goals!

"A plan without a goal is just a wish."

Goals! by Brian Tracy brings about a solution to this poignant problem statement. Beautifully articulated, *Goals!* answers the trivial question of why some people achieve goals and others don't.

Putting forth the right way of how to set goals and achieve them, Brain helps you get everything you want. With simple, practical and powerful methods, get ready to turn your wishes into being with *Goals!*

The author Brian Tracy is a bestselling author and motivational speaker. An expert on the subject of human potential and personal effectiveness, he has more than seventy books to his credit.

Book 2: Aligned Thinking

Empowering organizations, professionals and entrepreneurs, Jim Steffen, designer of the industry's most powerful management tools, aligned thinking and successful partnering, shows the way to live every moment and make it count with *Aligned Thinking.*

Combating the daily struggles of work-life balance and unraveling the MIN secret, the book reveals how you can make life the celebration it was meant to be.

Book 3: Work Reimagined

Richard J. Leider and David A. Shapiro, ardent teachers of finding your true calling and purpose of life, have authored 5 books together on these disciplines.

Their book *Work Reimagined,* a Silver Nautilus Award recipient, explores the concept of 'our calling'.

Answering probing questions of "What do I do? What do I really do? What is my real work?", *Work Reimagined* helps you discover what you should be doing in life.

Mixed with dozens of inspiring stories featuring people who have found or are in the process of finding their own calling.

Book 4: Courage Goes to Work

Going against the tide of being comfortable, complacent and too afraid to do things differently; "Courage goes to work" proposes a bold antidote: Courage.

With a step-by-step guide, Bill Treasurer, the author of this book, encourages modeling courageous behavior. Making the concept more concrete, he presents the three buckets of courage, illustrated with real-life examples and proven practice to keep these buckets full the whole time.

Bill's insights on courage and risk-taking have been featured on a number of platforms touching so many lives. His corporate programs have packed participants with courageous leadership, better team performance and more career backbone.

Book 5: Choosing the Right Thing to Do

David A. Shapiro is a writer, consultant, and educator. Starting his writing journey with script writing for stand-up comedians, he found his way to corporates.

Every day. All day long. We are presented with choices. And every choice that we make makes us who we are. In all of this, what is the moral legacy we want to leave behind?

"Choosing the Right Thing to Do" is a moral guidance compass for all ages without moralizing. Packed with real-life examples, the book helps to handle those tricky day-to-day problems. The heart of the book, choices defining character, tells the tale where we all want to do the right thing, but knowing what is the right thing isn't always going to be easy.

Taking you through the moral spectrum, across themes, *Choosing the Right Thing to Do* is a solution to making the right choices.

Book 6: Collaborating with the Enemy

In unity lies strength. Take it as fate may have it or ironically but true, if you want to succeed you will need to work with people you just don't like or trust. Adam Kahane, a strategist and facilitator, helps people work on these most important and intractable issues seamlessly.

In *Collaborating with the Enemy* he has penned down a ground-breaking approach that embraces discord, coexistence and acceptance. Collaboration, an inevitable value, makes you reach mid-way to make things work.

Book 7: Making the Impossible Possible

Set in the 50s, a tale of reaching the impossible finish line, *Making the Impossible Possible* reiterates that nothing in the world is impossible with unwavering efforts.

An example of excellent execution, problem solving and addressing difficulties, it is a story of Rocky Flats' mission of nuclear waste clean-up. A task that nobody believed would be completed ahead of schedule with profits, this story will move you with their outcome of extraordinary performance.

Written by Kim Cameron and Marc Lavine who have worked on organizational studies, this book is a must read for all leaders out there.

Book 8: Get There Early

The mark of a true leader is the ability to look into the future. Forecasting the opportunities and threats and designing today to compete to win.

Bob Johansen, distinguished fellow of Institute for the Future, does forecasts for numerous organizations. Taking a cue for IFTF, his book *Get There Early* brings in a fresh perspective of VUCA world, making future forecasts clear, precise and fruitful.

Filled with techniques, stories and real-life examples, *Get There Early* is not about predicting but forecasting the future.

Book 9: The Empress Has No Clothes

"We all have self-doubt. You don't deny it, but you also don't capitulate to it. You embrace it." – Kobe Bryant

Capturing the real-life struggles of Joyce Roché and Alexander Kopelman's spellbinding collaboration, *The Empress Has No Clothes* is Joyce's journey to conquering the feeling of inadequacy and embracing success.

Addressing the impostor syndrome that inflicts many successful people, the book offers practical advice and coping strategies to realize your worth and live a doubt-free life.

Brutally honest and relatable, *The Empress Has No Clothes* will captivate you to take on this journey of embracing success.

Book 10: Fear Your Strengths

Disclaimer: Overusing your strengths may not always be advisable. Anything in excess, even your strengths, if not monitored, may become the reason for your downfall.

Fear Your Strengths by Robert E. Kaplan and Robert B. Kaiser exhibits the other side of your strengths of how they work against you.

As mind-boggling as it may seem, the book gives you a glimpse of your strengths betraying you. Take a pause, calibrate your strengths and make them work for you.

For more in-depth reading, you can buy these books in paperback or ebook at https://www.bkconnection.com/